KATHLEEN MCCUE, M.A., C.C.L.S.,
WITH RON BONN

How to Help Children Through a Parent's Serious Illness

ST. MARTIN'S GRIFFIN NEW YORK

Design by JUDITH A. STAGNITTO

Library of Congress Cataloging-in-Publication Data

McCue, Kathleen.
How to help children through a parent's serious illness : supportive, practical advice from a leading child-life specialist / Kathleen McCue, with Ron Bonn.
p. cm.
Originally published: New York : St. Martin's Press, 1994.
ISBN 0-312-14619-1 (pbk.)
1. Parent and child. 2. Sick—Family relationships. 3. Parents—Death—Psychological aspects. 4. Family psychotherapy. I. Bonn, Ron. II. Title.
[BF723.P25M33 1996]
649'.1—dc20 96-22605
CIP

First St. Martin's Griffin Edition: September 1996

10 9 8 7 6 5 4 3 2

To my sister, Marjorie; may she
have as much faith in herself
as she's always had in me.

KATHLEEN MCCUE

For Dan, Dave, Julie, June, and Kathleen,
who taught me all I know on the subject.

RON BONN

Contents

Acknowledgments

Many individuals contribute to a project such as this, and they all have my deepest gratitude and respect. But there are a few special people who, over the years, have had a significant role in making a group of random ideas and concerns into first a service, and then a guidebook. Michael Kahn and Elliot Aronson showed me that my niche was children, and I am grateful. Extra thanks go to Margie Wagner, who taught me about the relationship between children and health care. The importance of teamwork emerged from the feedback of the early child life staff at Children's Hospital of Los Angeles. The writings of the Association for the Care of Children's Health, and the constant emphasis on parents as partners, made the phrase "family-centered care" become the core of my work.

More recently, Alice Scesny provided the support and leadership necessary to make good ideas into a real program and keep it going. Thanks to Shirley Gullo and Amy Weiss, nurses who provide a level of patient care and human concern that never ceases to amaze me.

Most important, the tough work was done by the hundreds of families who allowed us to have a role in their lives. Some of the children who contributed concretely to this book are Jennie Crook, Lea Crum, Sadie Mau, and Jessica Rottenberg, and I will always be grateful that they were willing to share part of themselves in the hope of helping others.

FOREWORD

My wife died of breast cancer in 1977, after a three-year struggle. When I came home from the hospital and told my two young children the tragic news, they were relieved when they realized we would all stay together. "We thought we'd be adopted," they said. I realized then how little I had prepared them for what would be the worst event of their lives. Shuttled back and forth between grandparents, they understood only that something was gravely wrong, that their world was coming apart.

As I read *How to Help Children Through a Parent's Serious Illness,* it all came back. I just wish this book had been available then. Remarkably insightful, it will be a gentle hand to help those who otherwise would have to face personal tragedy alone.

I thought no one could understand terminal illness within a family without having been there. Well, Kathleen McCue has been there.

I hope you never need this book but, if you do, use it, trust it. It could help your children for the rest of their lives.

—BILL KURTIS

PREFACE

A Quick Look Forward

The aim of this book is to help you help your children, from the moment a parent is diagnosed with a serious or life-threatening illness, or the moment you begin *looking* for help, right through the resolution of that illness, whatever that resolution might be. We may find ourselves together for weeks, months, or years.

If, however, you've picked up the book for help with an immediate problem or an emergency with your children, here is a quick guide to what each chapter contains. (At the end of most chapters, you'll find more detailed subject listings, to take you directly to whatever page you may need):

Chapter 1, "The First Day of the Rest of Your Life," starts from the moment of diagnosis. It explains what and how you should tell your children about the illness, what questions they'll probably have, how children of different ages are likely to react, and how you can help them. The central message of this chapter and of the book is absolute honesty.

Chapter 2, "Getting It Together," helps prepare your family for the long haul. It discusses how to minimize stress on the well parent; how to rally and organize the help that's available; what kind of help you can expect from your children, and what kind of help they'll need from you.

Chapter 3, "Early Warnings," details the early warning signs you may see when your children *aren't* handling the crisis. It explains how to look for signs of trouble in their drawings and their play, a series of specific warnings in behavior—sleeping, eating, school failure, and more—and how you can begin to handle them: what to ask and what to say. It warns strongly against permitting any pattern of failure to develop. The final section deals with children who seem to be trying to injure themselves.

Chapter 4, "Help! How to Give It, Where to Get It," goes into much more detail on how you can help your children when they show you they're in trouble. It covers how to understand what the trouble is, how to decide whether a child needs outside help, the different levels of help available—friends and family all the way up to psychotherapy—and where and how to find it.

Chapter 5, "Preparing Children for Hospital Visits," explains how to prepare children for visiting a sick parent: how to ready them for the frightening sights and how to decide whether a visit is a good idea or not. The chapter explores how to take children through two entirely different situations: a parent in intensive care and a parent hospitalized for a serious but non–life-threatening condition.

Chapter 6, "Coming Home," offers the briefing I give a well parent when the sick parent is about to come home—how to prepare your children, how to involve them, how to deal with their too-glowing expectations; the need to avoid big celebrations; what the well parent and the sick parent can expect from their children; and what the children will need from both of you.

Chapter 7, "When It Won't Get Better," deals with illness that will not go away—chronic, degenerative diseases that will persist or grow worse over years. It explains how to help your children understand what such an illness feels like and to cope with the permanent change in your family's life and adapt to this partial loss of a beloved parent.

Chapter 8, "When Things Get Very Bad," looks at dying, and living. Some of the subjects: children's last times with dying parents; to visit or not to visit the hospital; dying at home; legacies of love—on paper or on tape—that can live on in your children's lives after you leave them; and how the surviving parent and the children can help each other through their grief to an undamaged future.

Chapter 9, "Dealing with Special Family and Medical Circumstances," looks into special family or medical situations that may affect how the principles of the book apply:

- The single parent
- When the patient is *not* a parent
- AIDS
- Mental illness
- Contagious diseases
- Hereditary diseases
- When the child had a role in "causing" the parent's condition

A Special Note for Single Parents: In Chapter 9, under the heading, **If Yours Is a Single-Parent Family,** you'll find important suggestions for selecting a special friend or relative who can help you and your children through this medical crisis.

I suggest you read that section carefully, now, and begin to decide whom you want to enlist for this crucial role. You and your helper should use this book together, with the helper taking the role of "well parent" for your children, from here on.

NOTE TO THE READER: *The family stories that appear throughout this book are based on my case notes. I did not record conversations with children, parents, and medical professionals. Therefore, the conversations that accompany the stories are reconstructed and reported to the best of my memory.*

All of the names and certain characteristics have been changed to protect the privacy of those people with whom my work as a child life specialist have brought me in contact. I also note that many of the stories included in this book are composites, based on two or more real case histories.

A Reader's Forethought

Dear Ms. McCue and Mr. Bonn:

I am convinced it was an angel that led me to your book in the patient/family "library" in the gift shop in the hospital where my husband was being treated.

I couldn't sleep one night and began to read your truly extraordinary book. I read your suggestions for what was age appropriate for my sons, and discussed them with my sons the next morning (which was exactly two weeks after my husband had been admitted). I told them that their father's illness wasn't anyone's fault, it wasn't contagious, etc.

Three hours later my son Sam's eyes filled with tears (this is a child who *rarely* cries—even when physically hurt). He began, "You know, Mom, I asked Dad to play basketball with me and he told me he was too tired. I asked him again, and even though he only did the rebounds . . . and THEN HE WENT INTO THE HOSPITAL!" at which point he really started to cry.

Needless to say, for two weeks my son had carried the burden and responsibility of feeling he was responsible for his dad being hospitalized. Your book, with its guidance, anecdotes, and concrete, empirical suggestions not only alleviated the obvious pain and guilt of one nine-year-old child but also helped me lay the groundwork for an ongoing avenue of communication that continues to this day. Within the last two weeks, we have discussed everything from illness to God, etc. My son and I have forged a wonderful bond and relationship that was unthinkable and inconceivable to me only a few weeks ago.

Not only am I a parent, but I am also an educator by profession. Your book is clear, concise, "reader-friendly," and I am sure will aid countless other families in the future.

My family was blessed to have been able to be helped by your book and we will always be grateful. I have extolled the virtues of your book to countless professionals in the past few weeks (and I have spoken to many). In fact, I am buying a copy for my son's school to have for future reference. I hope and pray that your book becomes a mainstay in every library and every school so that if (God forbid) other families should need it, it will be there for them.

Thank God, our story appears to have a happy ending—we hope my husband will be home within a few weeks—and that he will continue his recovery at home and resume work, fatherhood, etc., with the same gusto and *joie de vivre* as he enjoyed in the past. In the meantime, my sons and I will be different, stronger, and better able to communicate and weather whatever storms the future may have in store for us.

So once again, from the bottom of my heart, a sincere thank-you. May you live to enjoy a full and healthy and happy life!

—Jane and Josh, Sam and Matt

Introduction

This book began without any of us realizing it.

As resident child life specialist at the Cleveland Clinic Foundation, I'd get a call, usually from the intensive care unit:

A child has come in, seen his mother or father lying in a bed, pale as death, hooked into a battery of life-support drips and monitors, and the child has gone berserk, run screaming down the corridor. Could I come?

Or the child is sitting stiff and silent outside the ICU, refusing to speak. Could I come?

Or the child is behaving perfectly well, only the nurse thinks he should be crying his heart out. Could I come?

These things happened again and again; they happen in every big hospital. But gradually we came to realize:

As surely as the parents of sick and dying children need help and support, *the children of very sick parents need help and support.* Yet while almost every good hospital has a continuing program for parents of sick children, *there didn't seem to be any programs to help children whose mothers or fathers were seriously ill.*

With all our advanced techniques for treating serious disease, for saving or prolonging life, we in medicine have forgotten one very important affected group: the children of our patients.

We have a great deal of knowledge about children and stress. Yet there was no organized effort to pass that knowledge on to the parents, *to help them help their children*.

In most hospitals no counselor, no manual, was routinely at hand to tell parents what to expect from their children and to work with the children, from the moment of diagnosis through months or years of a parent's treatment. There was no continuous guidance on how to address children's questions and fears, from the darkest puzzlings about separation, change, pain, and death, to the most mundane worries of "Who'll tuck me in? How will I get to soccer practice?"

There was no day-to-day counseling for the sick or the well parent on how to interpret their children's conduct and how to help children who were showing signs of trouble. What is "normal"? What is dangerously *not* "normal"? What signs can you look for? What warnings do children give? What can you say and do to maintain the mental and emotional health of your children through months or years of medical crisis, no matter what the final outcome?

Your Children: Part of Your Treatment

Out of that realization has come first our program and now this book.

From 1987 until 1995, if you, a parent, were admitted to The Cleveland Clinic with a serious or life-threatening illness, then as part of your treatment, at no additional charge, your children were entitled to our continuing services in the Child Life Program. Over those nine years we worked with hundreds of families. We helped well over a thousand *normal* children survive and prevail through a terribly *abnormal* situation in their lives.

In September 1995, this program was changed—another casualty of the general downsizing of medical care delivery in America. Although still committed in spirit to the needs of these youngsters, Child Life services for the children of severely ill adults are now available only on a very limited, consulting basis. As a result of continuing requests, a new program is now being discussed that would once again make our program available to help children of very sick parents. However, in order to survive the threats of cost containment, there will be a charge to families using the program.

Yet even when the children of Cleveland Clinic patients still had access to our free Child Life program, for other parents across America the problem remained: There was no guidance on how to bring their children through these devastating family medical crises. Even in our institution, parents had nothing in print they could routinely consult whenever they wondered about their children's reactions, their emotional well-being.

What was needed, I felt, was a *manual*—a book that would summarize the very best of our own and others' expertise, and guide Mom and Dad step by step through all the many turnings of how children respond to a parent's serious illness.

Perhaps, as you read this, you are thinking, "She's not really talking to me. *My* illness is treatable, it's curable." Please think again. If the illness is serious, if it will change you in some way, if it is causing you high levels of worry or stress, then it *will* affect your children.

Most of you who read this will survive your medical crisis, and return to a full, normal life. For you the aim of this book is to bring you and your children through even stronger, united, and ready to challenge the future. But please indulge me for just one moment: I want to tell you a story that involves a death. I tell it now, because it seems to me to make two vital points:

1. **Even in the face of ultimate tragedy, children can be prepared, can weather the trauma, can emerge whole and healthy and ready to go on with life.**
2. **On the other hand, children who are not prepared, not given the kind of support and understanding we'll be talking about throughout this book, can be permanently scarred by a parent's medical crisis, *even if the parent survives and returns eventually to full health.***

A Family Returns

You may remember it from the NBC Television report about our program.

Nine months earlier, a young mother I'll call Samantha Marks had died, after a long struggle with cancer. I'd been seeing her daughters—Annie, nine, and Carlie, six—all through her illness and after her death. But today was the first time their dad felt strong enough to return to the hospital where his wife had died.

Here is what he told the television audience about Annie and Carlie, and about Samantha's death:

"I told the kids the next morning. They cried for, I would say, a good twenty minutes. But then they—it seemed like they were prepared for it. Then they started comforting *me*, instead of losing it as I thought they would."

Annie said this:

"She never goes out of my mind. But sometimes I'm not thinking about her; I'm having a good time. But she never left my mind."

I said, "She never leaves your mind, but it's okay for you, right, to have a good time, and play, and have friends, and laugh?"

Annie said, "Yeah. *That's what she probably wants us to do.*"

At our very first meeting, Samantha herself told me she thought she could let go of life a little more easily, knowing her children would be helped and supported through her death and afterward.

Helping You to Help Your Children

If you are reading this manual, something terrible and frightening is happening to your family. It is happening to you, it is happening to your partner, and it is happening to your children, and you're worried about them. You want them to come out strong and sound, ready for future happiness and success, whatever the medical outcome.

There are no "right" answers, but there are answers—there are questions your children will certainly ask; there are reactions, healthy and unhealthy, that you can observe and deal with. There are situations you can handle and resolve, and there are signs that can warn you your child needs professional help. Age is an important clue to what children may think and feel, so some of our discussions will be divided into age groups. You can see where your own children fit in. Of course, there are no sharp dividing lines between groups.

This handbook is drawn from the great and growing body of knowledge of how children think and react, from our own years of experience and from the insights and experiences of other child health professionals. If, as I hope, this manual can help you now, please remember this:

It really belongs to all those other mothers and fathers who live with us, who have allowed us to share their struggle, who have died with us. Most of all it belongs to the children: the Survivors.

ONE

The First Day of the Rest of Your Life

PAY ATTENTION
TO ME.
Calvin and Hobbes
by Bill Watterson

You hear the words: "You have cancer." "You have M.S." "You have a brain aneurysm." "You need a heart transplant." The first thing you think about is your own life. And the second thing is: "What will happen to my children?"

Balancing Your Needs and Your Children's Needs

Here are two things that happened in our program at the Cleveland Clinic:

A young mother was being treated for cancer. She and her husband decided not to tell their nine-year-old son any details—too disturbing; why worry the boy? We'll just say Mom is sick; she'll be better soon.

But then the child began "acting out" in school—fighting with playmates, disrupting classes, falling behind. So the parents brought him to our program.

When I met him, the boy was grumpy—angry with his family, annoyed at being haled before a child life counselor. Yet behind all that he wanted to talk, and very soon he did talk.

He'd overheard his father on the telephone, speaking gravely with a relative. He'd heard the words "malignant melanoma" and suspected they had something to do with cancer. And he was furious. He explained why in three sentences: "They didn't tell me everything. She's *my* mother. I have the right to know what's going on."

The boy was absolutely correct. And what he said points up one of the central themes of this book: *The children of seriously or gravely ill parents always have the right to know what's going on.* Not only is that knowledge their right; it is one of their greatest *needs.*

The second story involves a father, a successful and self-assured businessman recently diagnosed with lung cancer. Once again, the parents decided not to tell their children, a nine-year-old girl and a six-year-old boy. The parents were pretty sure the children knew anyway, and they were right.

The children always know. Or, at least, they always know *something.*

The normally cheerful little girl was constantly sad, suddenly breaking into tears. One night she begged her mother, "Whatever you do, tell me the truth. Tell me Daddy's going to be okay." Neither realized that the little girl was asking for two different things. So the mother did what she thought was right: She told her daughter something she wasn't at all sure of: "Of course he's going to be okay."

The boy's symptoms were even more disturbing: While previously he'd never shown much interest in toy guns and warfare, suddenly all his play was about killing. He ran around, indoors and out, making finger guns, shouting "Bang, bang, you're dead." Death was the constant message; of his sister he said, "I just wish she was dead." The boy was now totally indifferent to his father; it was as if the father were not there.

Counseling the parents, I told them what to me was obvious, and what is the central message of this book:

You must tell your children the truth.

We'll talk a good deal throughout this manual about why that's so. But for the moment, here are three reasons:

1. **Your children are affected by everything that happens in the family.**
2. **The more serious the situation, the more they will be impacted.**
3. **Lying to your children, in any way, will inevitably make things worse.**

But this father resisted; he was adamant that his children not be told of his lung cancer, *even though they obviously already knew.* And finally he told me why:

"Don't you understand? If I tell the children I have cancer, *that means I really do.* How can I fight this thing, keep a positive attitude, do what the doctors say I must do, if I acknowledge that?"

Like the reaction of the boy in the first story, the father's reaction was absolutely normal. For *anyone* diagnosed with a serious illness, the first thought is for the self: How can I live and fight; how will I handle the long, intense, perhaps painful course of treatment; how can I cope with the possibility, however unlikely, that I may not survive?

For a while, *everything revolves around the self.* Only afterward come thoughts of family, of how this most personal crisis may impinge on the people we love. Yet the needs of those loved ones, particularly of our children, are immediate and pressing.

(In this case we reached a compromise: The father agreed that his wife should tell their children the full truth about his lung cancer. But she would also tell them, "Daddy can't talk about it now." Frequently, in the first days and weeks after diagnosis, it is the well parent who must deal most directly with children's needs and questions. We found an acceptable interim solution, until the father could deal both with the disease and with his children—until he *can* "talk about it now.")

Two needs collide: the patient's need to do whatever it takes to try to survive (if that includes fantasy and magic, so be it) versus the child's absolute, inescapable right and need to know the truth. The tension between those two needs is where this book begins.

Making Your Children Part of Your Treatment

We believe very deeply that, when a parent is seriously ill, the children must be treated right along with the adult. Indeed, the children's treatment is *part* of the parent's treatment.

Ideally, treating your children begins on the day of diagnosis—the day you learn that you or your spouse has a serious, possibly life-threatening illness. That is the best moment to bring your children into the frightening picture.

But:

- It is almost never too late to start doing things the right way.

Specifically, whatever point you may now have reached in your family medical crisis, whatever has already happened that may be creating problems for and with your children, *right now* is not too late to start handling things better. And that's because:

- Mistakes made with love are easy to correct.

Avoiding the Biggest Mistake

The guiding principles, from the beginning to whatever the end may be, are *openness* and *honesty.*

Being honest can be painful. Nevertheless, dishonesty, even with the honorable goal of protecting the children, *may be the single biggest mistake you as a parent can now make.*

We are looking at the rest of your children's lives. If they are deceived, lied to, "protected" from the truth, they will learn a lifelong lesson of distrust. There may be nothing more important in their lives than that they continue to trust the two people they love most—the parent who is sick and the parent who will continue to care for them.

Counselors, psychologists, and psychiatrists see them in their thirties and forties. And they say, "Doctor, I can't love anyone." And so often, when you look back, there was a real break in that love during that person's childhood. Very often the break can be traced to the illness or death of a parent—a break never brought out and handled by the child.

Children Are Stronger Than You Think

There is one thing I count on absolutely in my work with families and that you can count on now: Your children love you. Because they love you, they can handle what is coming; they are much stronger than you think possible. What we must do now is build on that love and so build that strength.

As this medical crisis forces its way into your life and your children's, what we will try to do is maintain a sense of trust and continuity of parenting—so that, whatever happens, your children retain their trust in the world and in the people who care for them and care about them.

Three Things to Tell Your Children

Whatever your children's ages, what you are going to do at this point is:

- Tell them you are seriously ill.
- Tell them the *name* of your disease.
- Tell them your best understanding of what may happen.

(As we'll see shortly, being honest does *not* mean telling everything. Children can absorb different levels of complexity at different ages, and you are the best judge of what your own child can understand. What it *does* mean, simply, is never telling anything but the truth.)

Before we go on to *how* to tell children at different ages, let me tell you one story that illustrates *why* they must be told.

A young mother was diagnosed with cancer. It was a kind of chronic leukemia whose treatment causes few visible symptoms; the parents decided they'd spare their nine-year-old daughter the worry. All the child knew was that Mom was going to the hospital now and again to get some medicine, not even staying overnight. No big deal.

One night, about two weeks after the mother was diagnosed, her daughter woke up in the middle of the night screaming.

She couldn't move her legs.

The little girl was rushed to Children's Hospital and evaluated thoroughly. There seemed to be no medical reason for her paralysis. The pediatrician—fortunately, a very good one—asked the mother whether anything was going on in the family. A new baby, marital problems, a move to a new house?

Nothing like that, she said, but there is one thing.

The pediatrician, who'd had no idea the mother was ill, told her that she *must* tell her daughter about the leukemia, tell her *right now.*

So together Mom and Dad told her the truth: Mom has cancer. It's treatable and being treated. Mom honestly expects that she'll be okay. And we're sorry to tell you this while you're sick, but we thought you should know.

The little girl said, "I'm glad you told me. I knew something was wrong. *I thought maybe you were getting divorced.*"

Within twelve hours she began to move her legs; two days later she was discharged from the hospital and has never had a recurrence. She still doesn't understand why she became paralyzed, but she doesn't have to understand it. She just needed to be treated with honesty.

A child can imagine much worse things than the truth.

The Three Ages of Childhood

As we begin to talk about how and what to tell your children, we'll divide them, very tentatively, into three overlapping age groups. Here as elsewhere, though, remember this: *You are the expert on your own children.* You know how they react, how mature they are, how they handle tough situations. When you think something's wrong, *something's wrong.* Follow your instincts; usually they won't lead you astray.

The three age groups, which require somewhat different handling (though always within the framework of total honesty), are:

- **Toddler through preschool,** from about age two to six
- **Latency,** or school-age, from about five or six years to twelve years
- **Adolescence,** those terribly complicated teen years

Generally, the first and third group need the most delicate handling. Latency age is usually just that; the child's potentials are *latent.* He or she tends to be a little better adjusted, a little better able to cope, than an older or younger sibling.

But remember, there are no neat lines in children's growth or behavior; these age divisions are anything but absolute. Your child may, probably will, move back and forth between responses, may not even seem to fit his or her age group at all. These are general guidelines, and *wherever your child fits in is normal for your child.* And you, Mom or Dad, are the best judge.

Think about how we might tell a youngster in each group that a parent is seriously or gravely ill.

Explaining Your Illness to Your Preschooler

The family: father, mother, six-year-old boy, three-and-a-half-year-old boy. The father was diagnosed with a brain tumor.

The younger boy was bright, verbal; his parents thought he could understand the situation. Each time we met, both boys were present. Naturally the big brother was the little one's hero and role model. If the big boy looked sad, the little one knew he should look sad, and did.

At the first meeting, we talked about the brain and how it was like a computer, how it ran everything else. Both boys understood that and how important it was. You could tell by watching their faces.

We maintained their concentration, particularly the younger boy's, by keeping everything very short—get the computer idea across, then play a little. With young children, that's extremely important; they can understand, but their attention span is like a hummingbird's.

And playing can be a marvelous tool. Take a doll or a stuffed animal. Say, "This is Daddy. Daddy's very sick. What's the matter with Daddy?"

Use the language your child uses. If an injury is a booboo, talk about booboos:

"Daddy's got a booboo."

"Where?"

"Up here, in his head."

Take a nice bright Band-Aid, stick it on. "The doctors are going to try to fix Daddy's booboo."

A parent can use a doll or stuffed animal just as well as a psychologist can. If the sick parent can do the explaining himself or herself, that is simply wonderful for the child. Hard on the parent, perhaps, but good for the child. And perhaps good for the parent as well. If you are the one facing that gravely uncertain future, everything you can do for your children will probably add to your own comfort. That's a thought we'll keep coming back to.

There's a difference between the three-and-a-half-year-old and the six-year-old. The parents told the older boy a little about the planned surgery, about the fact that the doctors were going to make an incision into Daddy's head to try to make him better. The younger boy wouldn't have understood about the incision; we left that out. Remember, being honest does not necessarily mean telling *everything,* where the child isn't ready to understand. It means never telling anything but the truth.

(In later chapters we'll talk about infants. You can't "tell" them what's going on. But in some very simple, important ways, you can make sure their world remains warm and secure in the midst of crisis.)

"I Think I've Ruined Her Life"

Before we leave this earliest age group, let me tell you one of the stories that gives me my absolute conviction: It's never too late to get things right for your children.

A young husband was beginning radiation therapy for lung cancer. In the corridor outside the treatment room, a nurse discovered his wife, sobbing. The nurse asked what was wrong. The woman murmured something about a five-year-old daughter. Then, quite clearly: "I think I've ruined her life."

The radiology people called me. I asked the mother what had happened. This was her story:

The family had not told the little girl anything about her father's illness. Five years old, they thought, was just too young. The morning before, Sunday, the family had gone to church. And the little girl had lit a candle and said this prayer: "God, please make Daddy's cancer go away, so Mommy will stop crying."

Mom and I sat and talked in the corridor for an hour. I told her what she might tell the little girl about her husband's cancer:

- Daddy has a bad sickness.
- The sickness is called "cancer."
- The doctors are treating Daddy now, and Daddy and I truly believe he will get better.

I assured her that a five-year-old could handle the situation. And I suggested some questions her little girl would almost certainly ask, questions we'll consider in the next section.

Afterward, the three of them went home and held a family meeting. They cried a lot, but they talked it all through, honestly. The mother called me several weeks later and said: "That was all we needed. We're communicating."

I never saw the little girl. I didn't have to.

Three Inevitable Questions

Sometimes I can predict the future.

I met with a father about to undergo radiation therapy for cancer. He had two children in the preschool and school-age range. I told him they would inevitably have three immediate worries that he and his wife would have to confront:

1. **The children would suspect that somehow, by something they had done or hadn't done, they had "caused" his cancer. This is called "magical thinking"; we'll meet it again and again. Young children believe in their own omnipotence; what happens around them happens *because of them. They can be overwhelmed by feelings of guilt for a situation totally outside their control.***
2. **The children would be afraid the illness was contagious, that by being with the parent, they too could "catch" cancer.**
3. **The children would want to know who would take care of them, who would do the "Daddy things" while Daddy was sick.**

The father called me several weeks later and said, "I can't believe my kids did all three of those things you said they'd do." Not all at the same time or the same place, but in those weeks, all three of those questions came up repeatedly. *They are the three universal concerns of children in those years.*

The Three Right Answers

How do you handle the three universal concerns? Head-on, with unequivocal answers. And be prepared: They'll come up again and again.

You don't need to go into detail for the first two questions; what you can say is something perfectly straightforward, along these lines:

"We don't know much about cancer. I don't know for sure how I got it. But I do know two things:

"*Nothing you ever did made me get it.*

"You can't get it from me. No one else can catch this cancer. This is something that's going to affect just me."

For the third concern, you *will* want to go into detail. And you'll want to give it some thought.

Remember that, especially for younger children, *routine equals security.* The family's routine is about to be disrupted, and you want to keep the disruption to a minimum for your children. Think about how you'll maintain their routine: who'll baby-sit when Mom takes Dad to the hospital; how will your children get to and from band practice, basketball practice, the party on Saturday night. Tell them, in detail.

At the same time, reassure your children that they have a role to play in taking care of the sick parent. In the next chapter we'll talk about what some of those roles may be, but remember: *They're entitled to help.*

Explaining Your Illness to Your Six- to Twelve-Year-Old Children

In addition to wanting answers to the three inevitable questions, this latency-age group is going to want some detail about the illness. Starting at about age six, children become intensely interested in bodies, their own and other people's. You can expect some pretty close questioning as to exactly what is wrong with you and what the doctors are going to do about it.

Tell the truth, without embarrassment. And try to get medical personnel to cooperate.

Want to See?

Ask the child: Would you like to see how the doctors are going to try to help Mom or Dad? Most young children jump at the chance; some of the older ones are a little more leery. Don't press; the child must *want* to go and see.

When a parent in our hospital is to receive radiation treatment for cancer, or is awaiting an organ transplant, our therapists encourage them to bring their children along to the evaluation session. That's when the technicians and the nurses show the children all around the floor, explain how the doctors and nurses will be taking care of Mom or Dad. Often they'll take a doll or stuffed animal into the treatment area and "treat" it just as they will the parent.

If the intensive care unit is available, I like to take the children there, to get an idea of what will be done for Mom or Dad and to get the children accustomed to what goes on, so they'll be prepared and will understand what's happening when their own parent is lying there, surrounded by drips and monitors.

All this is important right now, but it's also important in the long run: Whatever the outcome of the parent's treatment, the child who receives this kind of respect and understanding is less likely to resent and fear medical professionals, less likely to resist treatment and so jeopardize his or her own life years from now.

Explaining Your Illness to Your Teen-Agers

On the other hand, sometimes you *can't* predict the future. Usually the first thing I say to the parents of adolescents is, "If I could predict how your teen-ager will respond to this, I'd be a miracle worker. Nobody *ever* knows how a teen-ager will respond."

The fact is, a teen-ager facing a parent's illness may go off in all kinds of different directions, and that's okay—that's normal.

A parent's grave illness brings demands that most teens don't even begin to know how to handle. As adolescents, they're struggling to move away from the family. Now what should they do—move back and help, or run as fast as they can in the other direction? A parent's illness can create acute levels of psychological and emotional conflict.

Information, Please

Most adolescents seem to need an enormous amount of information; they want to be treated pretty much as adults. Not only will they want the basic information of the diagnosis, but they'll ask as well for the technical terminology, statistical information on survival rates; the depth of their questioning may astonish you. And you mustn't duck.

Keeping the Faith

Of all the age groups, adolescents are the most sensitive to deception and dishonesty—the most likely to lose faith in adults. In a way, *they want to lose faith in adults*—it's part of that normal process of moving away, into their own adulthood. So it's very easy for them to pick up an evasion or a white lie and say, "Well, Dad's a liar; I'm not going to believe anything he tells me."

Privacy: Theirs and Yours

Privacy is a very important issue to teen-agers; you can't force yourself inside their heads. You give the information and then wait: They may or may not talk to you. What's important is that they have *someone* to talk to. So if you know your teen talks from the heart to a best friend, the parent of a pal, a teacher, a coach, a minister or rabbi, then encourage him or her to share this new crisis.

But there's another consideration here: your own privacy. Probably you do not want the news of your illness "spread all over town." And you have every right to set guidelines: It's *your* family, *your* body, *your* illness. On the other hand, your teen-ager *must* have someone other than you to talk to. Keeping in mind those two sets of needs—your need for privacy, your teen-ager's need to talk—is there someone you can personally share your crisis with, explain that your child knows what's happening and may want to talk?

If you particularly do *not* want your son or daughter talking to teenage friends, *then you must be very clear about that from the outset*—and you must give the child another outlet. A teen's natural behavior is to go to other teens.

You can say quite honestly: "This is a very private illness. I don't want everyone in town talking about me. I'll be embarrassed if people treat me differently. So: I love you, I want you to know the truth, I know you need to talk, and here's who you can talk to. But I don't want this all over town, at least not yet."

This is not dishonesty. It is family privacy. And it's perfectly all right.

Giving Your Children Hope

However grave the illness, hope comes along with every diagnosis. And it is neither wrong nor dishonest to pass this hope along to your children. Your physician may tell you there is a 15 percent chance of survival. That gives you a *chance;* there is treatment and you're determined to make the most of it. Other people have licked this thing, and you will too. That is what, being totally honest, you can tell your children. Give them *your understanding* of what's happening and what can happen.

If you tell your children what you yourself truly believe and hope, even if there's a somewhat different spin from what the doctors have said, then there is no dissonance; it fits. Only when you tell them something you *don't* believe does the dissonance overwhelm their security and their confidence in you.

Fears of Dying: First Thoughts

Faced with the news of a parent's grave illness, all but the youngest children are going to wonder: *Will you die?*

They may or may not ask the question. They may ask it now or months from now. Nevertheless, however far the idea may be from your own thoughts, you must be prepared for the question. And to be prepared, *you need to know what your child thinks death is.*

A two- or three-year-old child may talk about death, may have a sense of its sadness. But the very young child could never really discuss it, never understand its consequences—above all, its finality.

By the time a child is at the middle of school age, around nine, ten, or eleven, he or she has come to grips with the central idea of death.

Most children know, by this age, that death is final, that you don't return from it, and that it is inevitable. It will happen to everyone.

Having an ill parent, who may die, probably forces children to tackle the issue sooner than they might otherwise. So what do they need from their parents?

They need to understand their parents' beliefs about what death is and what may or may not come after. That means, for one thing, you will have to understand and be able to articulate your own beliefs. And, whether the subject comes up immediately, on that day of diagnosis, or months later, you will want to be careful.

Marcy's Monster

Above is a picture, and its story:

A young father had died of cancer. He'd been treated in a local hospital, diagnosed as terminal, and simply sent home, with no support for him, for his wife, or for Marcy, their eight-year-old daughter. It was appalling care.

A few days later, at home, he died.

The hospital staff had given the mother virtually no meaningful information; she hadn't known what to tell her daughter and so had told her nothing. Now, night after night, Marcy would wake up screaming; she was sleep-deprived, almost out of her mind with fear.

Because the child herself had once been a patient at our institution, we brought her into our program. In trying to find out what was wrong, I asked her to draw a picture.

What she drew was shocking: A little girl is alone in her bedroom. In through the window floats a demon figure. And then her story came out:

Marcy's father had once been in trouble with the law. It wasn't a major infraction; he'd been picked up and briefly jailed on a charge of driving under the influence of alcohol. But the family, deeply law-abiding and religious, had made a great fuss. And the little girl had picked up the idea:

When Daddy died, he'd go to hell.

Now the father she'd loved had become the monster of her picture. Every night, all night, she dreamed he was coming to take her to hell with him. She would try to run to her mother, but his fingers would aim a magic beam at her door, and it wouldn't open. She would dream she was pulling at the door, screaming, as her demon/father flew down to grab her. And she would wake up screaming.

In the end, we worked through it. The mother explained to the little girl that her father had been a good man, that she herself deeply and truly believed he was now in heaven. (They also worked past another piece of bad advice. Someone had told the mother it would be wrong to let the troubled little girl sleep with her. We decided, under the circumstances, it was okay, at least until Marcy felt more secure. Follow your own instincts, not other people's ideas.)

Feeling Free to Question

Above all, when the subject of death arises, your children will need the topic to be completely open, so that at any point from the first day on, they feel free to ask any question and have it answered honestly, without evasion, without embarrassment.

At some point, if a parent is truly at risk of dying, children need to understand the permanence of death and that someone who dies does not come back. It's acceptable, it's normal, for children to wish, to hope, to imagine that this time death will somehow be different. All you can do is remind them that it's okay to wish, but the truth of the matter is that when people die, they don't come back. And when your children are ready to make that leap, they will.

Something to Think About Now

All life is terminal. Even if one's own timetable is tragically shortened by a medical diagnosis, the end is not yet. There is still time, time for children and parents who love each other to make the most of. Don't try to shield your children from making the most of that time.

TELLING YOUR CHILDREN: A SUMMARY

All Children, All Ages (page 10)
Tell them these three things:

- Mom or Dad is seriously ill.
- The name of the disease.
- Your best understanding of what may happen.

Preschool Age (page 11)
Explain the disease on the child's level.

- Use dolls or puppets to help.
- Don't go past the child's attention span.
- Don't go beyond the child's ability to understand.

School Age (page 15)
Tell them three things, and keep telling them:

- Nothing they did caused the disease.
- They can't catch the disease from you.
- Who'll take care of their needs—who will do the "Mommy things" or the "Daddy things" now.

If possible, let them talk to the doctors and nurses and see where and how Mom or Dad will be treated.

Teen Age (page 16)
Give lots of detailed information; answer every question fully.

Make sure there is someone outside the immediate family with whom they can talk on a continuing basis.

Be prepared for anything.

TWO

Getting It Together

BOINGG!

She told me, "I feel like the rope in a tug-of-war."

She was a young mother; her husband was in the hospital, just beginning chemotherapy before a bone marrow transplant—he'd be there at least five or six more weeks. She looked terrible. And this is what she said:

"I feel like a rope, with a lot of tentacles coming out. My husband needs me available all the time. My in-laws and the people in my own family want information; they're constantly coming to me with questions and, 'Well, tell him this, ask the doctor that.' And the children need me more than ever before; there are three of them and they're pulling three different ways.

"And all these people have hold of these tentacles, and here I am in the middle, and I'm being stretched out in so many directions—I'm stretched as far as I can go. I don't even know how to pull back in; there's just nothing left. . . .

"Kathleen, I'm going to go BOINGG!"

So now, as you and your children begin preparing for the first, acute period of a loved one's illness, the primary aim of this chapter is to keep *you* from going "BOINGG!"

The Next Few Weeks or Months

We're talking now about how to cope with the first few weeks or months of a medical crisis, a time of intensive treatment and vast disruption of family life. (Chapter 7 deals with long-term chronic illness, when a parent's medical condition must become a *routine part* of your family's life.)

Once again, let me make a prediction:

You and your family have just undergone a terrific shock. One spouse has been diagnosed with cancer and must begin a tough series of radiation or chemotherapy treatments. Or the diagnosis calls for an organ transplant, and now the patient must wait—in the hospital or at home—until one becomes available. Or there's a brain aneurysm, a leaking blood vessel, calling for immediate, delicate surgery. You will find that this acute medical situation divides itself into two phases.

The First Phase

Whatever the diagnosis, the first phase—the first few days—will almost arrange itself. You'll find yourself putting your normal life on "hold." Of course the well spouse can have two or three days off from work—take a week!—to cope with the situation. If the kids are out of school for a couple of days, so be it. Family members rally round; they even come in from out of town to help in any way they can, or just to be there for you.

And then everything changes.

The Second Phase

You and your children must begin to settle in for days, weeks, or months of continuing crisis. The well parent has to go back to work; the kids must return to school. Some of the help disappears; family from out of town must go back home.

And yet the medical crisis is unresolved; the chemotherapy, the wait for a heart or liver or kidney, the delicate, frightening surgery and the slow recovery are *still at the core of your family's existence.* You and your children must find a way to take your lives off "hold" *amid a continuing crisis.*

The Roller Coaster

This period of adapting to the second phase of a medical crisis is one of the hardest for families; everything is new and everything has to be invented as you go. And now, for the first time, parents and children are going to encounter the emotional roller coaster ride of acute illness. The ups and downs are going to be wrenching at first; later on you and the children will become more used to them.

But right now you'll find that the patient feels good one day, lifting your spirits, then feels rotten the next, bringing everyone down. The prognosis will be optimistic, then pessimistic, then optimistic again. You, the well parent, will think you've finally got everything under control, and by the next morning all your careful planning will fall apart.

Families come to me in these early days, and they tell me how the unpredictable ups and downs are simply tearing them apart emotionally. And I have to say to them "*It's going to be like that. What you're going through now is the norm.*" This acute phase of a medical crisis is one of the hardest times for families, and it's what we're going to try to prepare for now.

Preparing Your Children

One of the first things you'll want to do is give your children a kind of warning: The sick parent *and the well parent* are going to be distracted, maybe a little shaky emotionally. Sometimes the children will find one or both of them grumpy. The children may feel ignored, and they may be right; at times neither parent will be able to pay attention. If you let your children know these moments are coming, and why, they'll handle them a lot better when they do occur. *Your children do want to help.*

Explain too that the relationship is going to be especially tough for the sick parent. Go into a little detail about exactly how that parent is feeling now. Yet even as sick as that, Mom or Dad is still your mom or dad and still wants to be involved in whatever happens in your life now. You'll have to cut each other a little slack.

Some Helpers to Relieve the Stress

First, let's see about snipping off some of those tentacles that can make you feel you'll go BOINGG. The fact is, some of those well-intentioned people who are stretching you can become part of the solution.

One of the quickest ways to find relief is to designate a *family communicator.* Draft a brother, sister, cousin, or grandmother to keep in touch with you and with all those circles of concerned relatives, friends, and acquaintances. Politely steer all calls for information, advice, and chit-chat to the communicator; explain that he or she will have the latest medical reports and will pass on messages to you every day. *Get yourself off the phone.*

There's another ally you probably already have: your phone answering machine.

"Hi, thanks for calling. John's latest medical reports look good; he may be up to some visiting next week. We really appreciate your interest but we're a little busy around here now, so please leave a message, and we'll talk later. I'll update this information every couple of days." Again, the important stuff will get through, but *you stay off the phone.*

And at some point you may simply have to tell it the way it is: Let friends and relatives know how stressed you are, and say: "We really appreciate your help and concern, but, please, *lay off us for a while.*" If you don't feel like saying that right out, perhaps your communicator or even a hospital social worker can do it for you.

Volunteers: Grab 'em!

So often a stressed parent will tell me at the beginning of a medical crisis, "Everybody *wants* to help, but nobody *helps!*" That urge to help is real; it can make your life right now a lot easier. It's also transient—after a while, it goes away. So now, at the beginning, is the time to grab it, focus it, and to put some lines out for the future.

Figure out specific things that will help, and ask for them. You're not imposing; people like to feel useful and, after all, they *did* bring it up.

- "Could you make a casserole?"
- "Gosh, I've got three loads of laundry sitting by the washing machine—could you possibly. . . ?"
- "It would be wonderful if somebody could take the kids to McDonald's tonight. . . ."

All of this can provide immediate relief and help bring you back to your center. And a little more thought can extend the help into the future.

Remember, while the *will* to help is going to continue, people eventually stop *offering.* At first, when a family member goes to the hospital or comes home with a new disability, people rally round to offer assistance. That outpouring usually doesn't last too long; after a while, people sort of fade back into their own lives and you'll find yourself living alone with the crisis.

So in those first, generous days, try to think of some of the help you'll need *in the future* and start to put some strings on it. The outpouring is there: grab it! "We're in good shape right now, but soccer season starts in two weeks, and Danny's going to need some rides; may I call you then?"

It may be a little difficult to think that far ahead, but anything you can take care of now, while friends and family are eager to help, will certainly pay dividends in the future—when, three days before Danny's first game, you can simply pick up the phone and say, "Hi. Remember your nice offer to drive Danny. . . ?"

As Time Goes By

Of course you can't think of everything in that first, frantic week or two. You're going to continue to need help. Probably, as days become weeks and months, you'll receive fewer and fewer offers. Yet that helping impulse is still there; it's just that people are thinking about other things. Those tentacles are still tugging at you, though, so now you have to reach out for the help. Many people are a little timid about *asking* for help, and that's unfair to the helpers: They *want* to be there for you. Helping makes people feel good.

And if you're still shy, think of getting someone else to ask for you. That's where the professionals at your hospital can come in: We're pretty brazen about asking help for our clients!

"How Would You Feel . . . ?"

I met with a young couple. The mother was beginning chemotherapy for her cancer. First, of course, we talked about their own two children and the need to be absolutely truthful with them. They agreed on a family meeting to do that. But then, as I thought we'd about wrapped things up, she said:

"You know, there is something else I need to ask you: How about the rest of my family? I haven't told anybody about this thing, and I come from a big family: I have six brothers and sisters. But I don't know if I can tell people about it; *I don't want them to feel they have to do stuff for me,* and I don't want them to hang around looking sad all the time. I need them to be happy, not worried about me. I don't want them to be different."

It came pouring out, all the ambivalence about what to tell the family, and whether to impose—the same kinds of concerns you may be having right now. And after she got it all out, I asked her: "If this happened to one of your sisters, if she were dealing with this, and she didn't tell you, *how would you feel?*"

She said, "*I'd be furious.*"

And that, of course, was the right answer.

People diagnosed with serious diseases, and their immediate families, need support from the people who love and care about them. The love is there, the help is there.

So: If it happened to people you love, and they *didn't* call on you, *wouldn't you be furious?* In a sense, you owe it to your family and friends to let them in and let them help.

Everybody wins.

Getting Help from Your Children

Start with three ideas:

1. When the family is in crisis, most children want to help. But:
2. They want to do what they want to do.
3. The help you can expect will depend on your children's ages, their personalities, and your own family style.

You need to be creative about the assistance you ask from your children, and you need to make sure they still have time and space to do their own things.

The amount of help, the *kind* of help, will differ from child to child, age group to age group, family to family. It will depend on:

- The personality of each child
- The child's relationship to the sick parent
- The child's tolerance of the yuck quotient

One child's being helpful might be carrying out the emesis basin, while another's is just staying out of the way and not being too demanding. Both can be equally helpful, can chop off tentacles. Remember that children, whatever the task, *need to be praised for their help.* The praise will make them feel good and appreciated, and will encourage more help in the future.

Don't Assume

A lot of parents, in my experience, seem to assume their children will somehow *know* what's needed from them, *know* they have to be good now. *Wrong.* Children are by nature focused on themselves; their world revolves around them, and that world owes them growing up. Only as they do grow up will they become more outward-oriented, less self-centered.

It's very healthy for your child to be self-oriented and self-protective. But this means that, when your children are in that stage, any request for change is a big one, and their help should be praised. It should never be taken for granted.

A Promise

Before we go into the specifics of the help you can ask of your kids, let me make you this promise:

Your children have reserves of strength and character that you have never called on and never dreamed of.

Parental illness shakes up a family and provides an opportunity for new behaviors. *Some of those opportunities are wonderful;* they can actually help children to grow in ways they might never have grown without the crisis.

I've seen children become more self-sufficient, develop self-confidence and independence. I've seen brothers and sisters learn to get along with each other.

I've seen them learn to cook!

So a great deal of good for your children can come out of this crisis if you use them, encourage them, expect the help you need, and praise them for giving it.

Everyone Has a Job

Right from the beginning, make it clear to the kids: "In this time of trouble for our family, *everyone has a job.* Mom's job is to get treated and get well; anything beyond that, we'll all have to divvy up. My job as dad is to go to work and to be there for Mom and you kids.

"For you guys, the first job is school. Even with all that's going on here, even though you're worried about Mom, even though I'm going to need your help around the house: *The first job is school.* Mom and I expect that, no matter what's happening, you'll continue to work, keep up your grades, keep making us proud of you."

Help from Toddlers and Preschoolers

At this preschool age, the help is probably more *for* them than *from* them. Can your four-year-old tell time? Ask him to remind you when

Daddy needs to take his medicine. Send him in to ask Dad: What would you like to drink with the pills? Keep in mind: The child will want to do something that involves *direct contact* with the sick parent—asking him to vacuum the rug won't do it.

Help from School-age Children

At this age you can start to look for some real help. Get the children involved in the planning: Have a meeting with them and divide up the chores the sick parent can't do. Make a list together. . .

Mowing
Laundry
Pet care
Sorting the recyclables
Cooking
Doing the dishes
Washing the car
House cleaning
Shopping
Snow removal

Write down all the things that must continue to be done, medical crisis or no, then parcel them out among yourselves. You can start by asking for volunteers, then divvy up the jobs nobody really wants but that have to be done.

Help from Teens

The list is cumulative. So in addition to all of the preceding tasks, you can ask the teens to help care for younger siblings. This is a huge sacrifice—which is why, after some complaining, they'll feel very good when they do it, especially when you tell them what a terrific help they are.

But be prepared to head off the opposition:

"Aw, Ma, I don't want to stay with the little dork again."

"Well, it has to be done—do you have a better idea?"

"Sure. Hire a sitter."

"Honey, you know how tight money is right now, with Dad so sick. I really need you to do this. But—maybe I can do something for you?"

SAYING THANKS

Any little extra privilege is a good way to say thank you. Permission to stay up an extra half-hour weeknights. An afternoon of Nintendo at a friend's house, even *before* homework is done. An hour past curfew Saturday night.

Trying to Be the Grown-up

Sometimes, knowingly or not, a child will try to take on a parental role, almost seeming to step into the shoes of the sick parent. You may notice your child

- Becoming a disciplinarian for younger siblings
- Becoming overly protective and overly concerned for the *well* parent—assuming a role as surrogate wife or husband
- Becoming generally bossy, trying to run the household.

All this is a matter of degree, and both parents will have to make judgments. Taking on some level of responsibility is a good thing for a child and for the family in crisis; it's to be encouraged. But the parents must define a line that their children are not to overstep. Generally, children should be expected and encouraged to take over necessary *jobs* in the household; they should *not* be expected or encouraged to take over a parental *role.*

The well parent should make a mental check: Am I *expecting* my son or daughter to take on the role of semi-parent? If that's the case, the well parent must consciously back off from those expectations.

Try to avoid catchy phrases like "Well, Timmy, looks like you're going to be the man of the house for a while." And make sure well-meaning relatives don't lay that kind message on Timmy.

Even if a child must take on some kind of a parenting role temporarily, be very clear when that job will end: "I know, sometimes when

I'm away with Mom at the hospital, you *do* have to tell your little brother what he should and shouldn't do. But remember, that's just for now: when Mom comes home, she'll still be Mom. You won't have to be in charge any more."

It's wise to put that positive spin on the prospect, because sometimes children (just like the rest of us) don't want to give up authority. So it's important that they know, right from the start, that any grant of power is temporary. Mom will still be the mom; Dad will still be the dad. That's the best way for the whole family.

Help: How Intimate?

Just how helpful can your children be in actually caring for their bedridden parent? There's no absolute answer; what you can ask of them depends on your family's own style and your children's own sensitivity. Most children will want to be involved; they'll be both curious and interested in some of the intimate details of medical care.

Children are intrigued by medical equipment; they like to watch what's going on, and watching can lead to participation. Young children may like to sit there while you change the central line dressings or an ostomy bag for the patient. They'll want to hand you things, to "help." They won't necessarily want to *do* the hands-on things, but *they like to think they're helping in some way.* And as long as they're not getting in the way of proper medical procedure, that's fine—let them. But:

Don't push them to do anything they're uncomfortable with. If a child doesn't want to perform some intimate chore, and there's someone else available (including you), then get it done without the child. Over time, the child may *want* to get more involved, if you don't push now.

But if and when your child expresses an interest in helping with a personal function—emptying a bedpan, changing a bag—that's fine.

A Matter of Style

Think about your family style, with regard to privacy, intimacy, nudity. If you've taught your child that bodies are private and then you want her to change the pants on an incontinent parent, *you're violating what you've been teaching her all along,* and that's going to set up serious conflicts.

The family that sits in a hot tub together with little or no clothing on is going to have fewer boundaries than the family whose motto is "Shut the door."

Curiosity

Remember, *children are fascinated with bodies*—their own and yours too. Many children are extremely curious about surgery; they want to *see* what happened! This will be a matter of the *parent's* comfort level: If you can describe what the doctors did to you, so the child is prepared for what he's going to see, then "seeing" will probably be a good, uniting experience for both of you . . . an intimate memory to share.

What will probably happen is "Oogh, that's really gross!" and then you'll both be fine—down comes the shirt, and it's still the same old dad lying there. If the child doesn't ask to see, it's okay to offer.

More on Helping

When we find ways for the children to help—really help—we're doing the best job for them. It's not just chores. It can be little—or even pretty big—sacrifices: postponing a birthday party, or having it over at Grandma's house; nobody coming to Parents' Night; not enough money for band camp this year.

If your child's normal behavior is to slam doors, roar through the house, generally drive a sick parent crazy, then just acting differently—acting against what's normal—is a way for her to help.

Rather than follow your natural impulse, which might be to scream "Don't you know I'm sick? You're the most thoughtless child!" put it in a positive light:

"Look, just for a while, I need you to think about being quiet—not running, not slamming things. And that's going to be a big help." Anything that gives your child a concrete task to fulfill is going to make her feel great about herself, now and in the long run.

In a way, it's like training a puppy: A little praise is going to buy you a lot of good behavior. When a puppy happens to make his puddle where you want him to make his puddle, it's "Goooood puppy; oh, what a gooood doggy it is!" And when you notice that your child has done something helpful without being reminded, tell him, "I've been feeling so crummy; I couldn't even think about taking out the trash; it's *wonderful* that you did that!" Very few children—very few of the rest of us either—really hate being a bit overpraised.

Helping Your Children

That's how they can help you: Now, how can you help them? A lot of things about a parent's illness can make your kids go *BOINGG!* too.

In the next chapter, we're going to look for signs of trouble in your children. But here, at the beginning, we can try to head off the trouble.

Helping Your Infants, Toddlers and Preschoolers

For the smallest members of your family, the three most important issues are:

Security, security, and security.

From the moment of diagnosis, their house is not their home—not the home they knew. There's a flurry of activities; people coming and going; phones ringing and endless murmured phone conversations. It's all scary, and it's bad for your children's stability. And you can't really control it.

What you can control is *routine* and the security it represents. Try to keep your children on their old schedule:

- Preschool
- Mealtimes
- Naptimes
- Bedtimes

If *you* can't handle keeping the routines going, get help from the friends and relatives who can. Ideally, your *toddler's* life will stay the same; all the other stuff is grown-ups' problems.

Home and Away

At some point, you may have to farm your young children out for a while—you may have to spend days or weeks with your husband or wife at a hospital in a different city. Here again, the wisest course is the least disruption.

You'll probably have a lot of offers from friends and family to take your kids. *Pick one.*

There's a natural tendency to set up a rotation, to say "Well, Grandma can have them from Friday through Sunday, and then Cousin Marge will do Monday and Tuesday. . . " Your idea is not to impose too much.

But for the good of the children, you're going to *have* to impose.

For a baby, moving out of his own home is hugely disruptive. After that, every additional move is still more disruptive, and the pattern can have long-term consequences. Moved and moved again, your infant learns to distrust his environment. Just when he's taught one grown-up which cry means "I'm hungry" and which means "I'm wet," he must start all over again, training a new stranger. The lesson he begins to learn is "I can't really trust people to meet my needs."

Constant house-shifting during a crisis can damage a child's ability to trust and be close to others later in life. So when your kids—especially your littlest kids—must go away to somebody else's house, they should stay in that house until they can come home.

Doing it that way also chops off a couple of more tentacles for the future—you'll have more help available for the next time you need someone to take care of them, from all the folks you didn't impose on this time.

Helping Your School-age and Teen-age Children

For your older children, you'll want to make sure the school—which means teachers, guidance counselors, and school nurse—knows what's going on. These people will be your allies in watching over your children's emotional health and looking out for signs of trouble. Get them on board right at the start.

If your children will be living away from home, make sure the school people know that—your son or daughter won't be able to get back in the house for a while, won't be able to dig out old notes or use the family Macintosh.

Doing Their Thing

At the same time you and the children are divvying up the jobs that have to be done, you'll want to look out for another set of needs—theirs.

What's going on in their lives over these coming weeks and months? What has to be done to keep *their* routines going?

Are exams coming up? Will they have the time and materials they need for studying?

How is Tommy going to get home each Tuesday and Thursday after band practice? Who'll get Sheila to her girlfriend's birthday party on Saturday night, and who'll get her home on time?

And how about Sheila's own birthday, three weeks from now? Can she still have the party? Could we possibly switch it to someone else's house—that would surely be a big help!

Work together, with a datebook or one of those calendars that have big blocks to write in.

It's hard for kids to plan for the future, but now is a good time to get them started. They'll feel responsible—feel good—working with you to make up a schedule. And the better they get at looking ahead, the more certain it is that the things they want and need will still be there for them.

Thinking of You

When a parent is going into the hospital for more than a night or two, I like to suggest staying in touch with the children, just to let them know Mom or Dad is thinking about them. One way, of course, is little notes sent home from the hospital. But more than that: While you're packing, tuck away a few messages your kids can discover as the days go on. An "I miss you too" in a bookbag, or "Blow 'em away, babe" in a trumpet case or "Sorry I'm missing the game, but I'm rooting for you guys" in a gym bag can give that little lift, provide the occasional reassurance that you're still all together in each other's hearts.

For the younger kids, there are inexpensive little toys, with little love-ya notes, that can show up unexpectedly in the mailbox or under a pillow.

It really doesn't take much to maintain the bond, and these surprise love-taps will provide as much of a lift for you as for your children.

Doing *Your* Thing

All we're talking about is part of *parenting*—your children's central need; usually it's just automatic. But in this time of crisis, *you have to deliberately parent your children.* In the midst of all those tentacles pulling at you, you must stay conscious of their needs. And sometimes that's just going to get to be too much.

Take your children into your confidence. Tell them, straight out, that in order to help them, you must first help yourself—that means taking some time for yourself, taking time to rest, or making the simple decision occasionally to say "No."

And if, on occasion, you have to say "I can't—I don't have the time—I'm too sad," *that's okay.* Don't beat yourself up or think you're a terrible parent. That kind of honesty isn't bad parenting—it's good parenting. Your children *can* cope; they really are willing to live a day at a time. Knowing they're helping you makes them feel important and useful and grown up. And they *can* recover from a temporary lack of parenting.

Find someone to talk to: Nothing seems quite so bad or unmanageable once you get it outside your own head. Find a confidante among friends or family; talk with a friendly nurse or doctor. If the crisis is going to continue for a while, find a support group—sometimes listening to other people's troubles, and having them listen to yours, is the best therapy of all.

Life After *Boingg!*

Sometimes, under the kind of continuing stress you are going to be dealing with, the best of us snap . . . we do go *BOINGG!*

Usually for a parent, the snap comes not from doing too little but from trying to do too much—from refusing to recognize our own limits. That's what Callie did.

Callie had a twelve-year-old daughter: a tough age. Callie's husband had been discharged from the hospital after a severe first round of radiation and chemotherapy for his cancer. He still needed a lot of care, day and night; the doctors may have sent him home a bit early. I'd seen the mother and daughter while he was hospitalized, but not since.

One morning I got a call from the girl's school counselor: She was in his office. The night before she and her mother had had a terrible fight. It started small: Callie asked her daughter to bring some medicine; the girl had better things to do. Finally she brought the medicine and slammed it down on the beside table—whereupon Callie slapped her across the face, chased her out of the room, and slapped her again.

Pretty obviously, this was a family at its wit's end.

So, after talking to Callie (who was devastated by what had happened), the counselor and I got to work. I arranged for the father to be readmitted to the hospital; the constant care he needed was simply too much for his wife to provide at that moment.

The counselor arranged for the daughter to go stay with her married brother for a week.

Callie got a week without tentacles—a week filled with eight hours sleep a night.

Mother and daughter are both doing fine now—even though neither one is exactly sure what set off the explosion. Remember:

Mistakes made with love are easy to correct.

And sometimes everything has to escalate until a family faces the fact: "Wow, we are in big trouble." Then they can accept help.

Getting It Together: A Summary

After diagnosis, expect two phases in your family's life:

The first few days to a week, when you run on autopilot (page 25)
The second phase:

- Less help as helpers return to their own lives (page 25)
- Everyone on an emotional roller coaster (page 26)

It's vital to prepare your children for the emotional swings, the lack of parenting that lie ahead (page 26)

How to get the help you'll need:

- Appoint a family communicator, to keep relatives informed (page 27)
- Use your answering machine to keep callers updated and get you off the phone (page 27)
- Accept offers of help, and tell people what you'll need: a casserole, the laundry done, rides for the kids (page 27)
- Arrange help for the future (page 28)

Getting help from your kids

What kinds of help? (page 30)
How children grow under stress (page 31)

The help you can expect, by age group:

The youngest through preschool (page 31)

- Give them little jobs they can succeed at
- Don't look for deep understanding of what's going on

School-age children (page 32)

- Job one: Continue to succeed at school
- Divide the chores, and assign them fairly

Teen-agers (page 32)

- Job one: School performance still the priority

- Big help, big sacrifice: caring for younger siblings
- A fair sharing of household chores
- Caution: don't expect them to take on the role of the sick parent

Help from your children: how intimate? (page 34)

Giving your kids the help *they* need

Infants through preschool (page 36)

- Keep the number of caretakers to an absolute minimum
- Minimize change
- Maximize security

School-age children (page 37)

- Maintain normal activities and routines
- Provide regular updates on the sick parent
- Keep the school informed

Teen-agers (page 37)

- Encourage interaction with other teens
- Reward mature behavior with extra privileges
- Keep up normal activities and interests
- Keep the school informed

And sometimes, despite all this good advice, you'll just be overwhelmed. Some thoughts about that (page 39)

THREE

Early Warnings

Calvin and Hobbes **by Bill Watterson**

Moira Is Fine

The one thing Dad was sure of: Moira was fine.

There were four children, ranging from three to twelve years old. A few weeks earlier, Mom had been diagnosed with cancer. The family was close and loving; Mom and Dad had explained her disease to all the kids, each on his or her level of understanding. The medical prognosis was good. And as Mom began treatment in the hospital, Moira, the eldest, pitched right in, helping Dad with all the younger kids . . . almost a surrogate Mom. No problem there; she was being marvelously mature.

But he worried about the others; how were they handling it? Could he be missing some important signs with any or all of them? So he asked me to see them.

We divided them into two groups; I spent the first hour with the nine-year-old. I was impressed; he didn't talk much, but he knew what was going on with Mom, knew the children had Dad and each other to huddle with, knew Dad and Moira could do the Mom things. He gave Moira a lot of the credit.

Before he left, he drew a lot of pictures to give Mom next time they saw her. They took the pictures home.

A day or two later Dad brought in the three-year-old and the five-

year-old. Moira came too—because, she said, the little kids might be scared. When she introduced me to them, I got the feeling Moira was checking me out. Then she asked: While I played with the children, could she just sit and draw something?

The toddlers were a delight—outgoing and bumptious, with a lot of medical play, which showed me they pretty well understood what was happening to Mom and weren't afraid. No sign of insecurity anywhere. This father had done one heck of a job with his children!

Meanwhile, Moira had drawn a strange and lovely little picture. There were trees, flowers, a rainbow, color everywhere—and everywhere colored balloons, floating up toward the sky, becoming smaller as they drifted away. I asked Moira to sit on the couch with me and tell me about her picture.

"Oh," she said, "it's just a park."

"And the balloons? Tell me about the balloons, floating away?"

"Well," she said, "that's what happens. When something's real special, or real pretty, and you love it, it goes away and never comes back." And she burst into tears.

What Moira was telling herself, me, and anyone else who looked at that drawing was this: Moira was *not* "fine." Moira was good, helpful, no trouble at all; for parents in crisis, Moira was *easy.* But she was not fine.

Those tears, unlocked for her by her own picture, were her first release. She told me she was never sure she was doing a good enough job helping Dad with the other kids; she worried constantly about that. The others, she felt, were expecting her to do all the Mom things, and she didn't always know how.

Then as we talked further, some of the anger began to surface: It was *too much.* Too much was being expected of her by too many people; Moira wanted to do some of her own things as well. She was, after all, twelve years old.

At length I told her, "This is really important stuff, and your dad needs to know it—if the three of us sit down together, can you tell him?" Yes, Moira thought she could.

And we did, and she did. And her father, who'd been worrying about the other children, sat there astonished at what his oldest daughter was telling him. And then he took over:

"I didn't know you felt any of this," he told her. "You are not the mom in this family; Mom is Mom, and Mom will come home in a few days; she'll be sick, but she'll be your mother and my wife. As to you, you're my little girl."

And they cuddled while he told her this.

"As to the help we need," he said, "there's plenty available," and he listed the aunts and uncles they could call on to do "the Mom things." Moira would still be needed, of course; sometimes he'd need her to take care of the other kids, but if she had something special on, a party to go to or just friends to be with, then that would take precedence. They'd *make* it happen.

It's a true story, and it still makes me feel good—particularly since Moira's mother is doing fine after her breast cancer surgery. But it raises the questions we'll look at in this chapter:

- What kind of trouble may your children be having?
- How can you know? What are the signs of trouble?

Looking for the Patterns

First, let's throw out what we're *not* going to worry about. Almost never will we be concerned with one single act, one moment of time, however rotten. Terrible days are normal, as long as they don't happen every other day.

What we *are* going to look for are *continuing patterns of behavior* that tell us the children aren't handling the stress of Mom's or Dad's illness.

Any situation that interferes with your child's normal functions—school achievement, interaction with friends, eating and sleeping patterns—is abnormal. And the longer the abnormal situation continues, *the greater the potential for long-term damage.* And that's what we're really concerned with: spotting and cutting off these abnormal patterns *before* they begin to do damage.

No child can stand alone. Your children are part of a unit called family, and they will draw their strength from it as you draw yours. No child can make her own way through a family medical crisis; my own practice proves it to me every day: The children who emerge whole and healthy are the ones whose parents recognize how much of their children's emotional survival depends on them.

Pictures and play: How Children Communicate

Remember how Moira gave the first indication that she was troubled—more troubled, I suspect, than even she realized? With a drawing. Children, younger children especially, aren't very good at expressing themselves verbally. They tell us their really important secrets through what they do and what they create—through play.

There's a remarkable sequence in the NBC News "Sunday Today" report on our work. A young mother entered the hospital for gynecological surgery, with every prospect of success. And she wanted to be sure her daughters—Kara, age eight, and Jean, who was four, understood: *Mom fully expected to be all right.*

I started medical play with the girls, and as Jean was placing a catheter (correctly) in a doll, I asked, "Is she going to be okay?"

Jean shook her head. "No," she said.

I said, "She's *not* going to be okay?" Jean shook her head.

At this point Kara interrupted authoritatively, "Yes she is. She's going to be okay."

Jean stopped speaking . . . and a few minutes later, she picked up the doll and hurled it across our playroom.

You didn't need a degree in psychology; what happened was clear to anyone watching: Jean was announcing that she wasn't satisfied; she still doubted that the doll—that Mom—was going to be okay, and Kara had simply cut her off in middoubt.

I let Kara play with something else, then sat down face to face with Jean and said, "I really do think she's going to be all right now." I repeated the message in several ways, until finally Jean made eye contact and nodded agreement: Yes, she thought so too.

The message is very simple: Watch your kids, and listen to them. Watch and listen while they play; there are messages, and the messages aren't subtle.

- Watch for signs of fear and anxiety. Look especially for forms of play that weren't there before. Children who are worried about a parent's illness, particularly where surgery is involved, may begin to mutilate things, to tear up dolls, toys, Lego structures.
- Or toys may begin to disappear; a favorite doll isn't there any more. Why? "She doesn't like me." Such disappearances are frequently symptoms of the child's *fear of separation*—and again, the signs are not subtle.
- Watch for newly aggressive play, games of war and gangsters. A lot of anger may show itself in a sudden interest in death and killing.
- Listen to what they tell dolls, or stuffed animals, or imaginary friends, in those half-murmured conversations. In their play, is someone sick? Is someone dying? Is someone never coming back? Listen for problems:

  "I have cancer, and now you're going to get it too!"

  "You were a bad dolly, and now I'm sick—see?"

What to do? Probably it's best not to interrupt the games that are worrying you; let the child play them out. But afterward, you can open discussions: "I noticed you had the Mommy truck not come home—do you think I'm not coming home?"

You will need to reinforce those first key ideas from chapter 1 continually; they'll keep coming up in a dozen different ways. Remind your children:

Nothing you did made me get this.
There is no way you can get it from me.

Directing Their Play

Children always play, and they play the themes that are important in their lives. But high levels of stress and distraction, with a noisy, confusing home environment, may limit their play—and what you can learn from it.

Since children, especially younger children, express themselves more easily in play than in conversation, you as the parent may want to step in and *direct* the play, to see a bit deeper into those remarkable little minds.

You'll need to do what we do in our playroom:

- Establish a quiet atmosphere—your living room or the child's bedroom will be fine.
- Keep the stimuli down—no TV, no other people wandering in and out.
- Have just the parent or parents present, ready to be patient and play at the child's pace and direction.

You'll want to provide toys that let your children make up stories, especially stories around the areas that concern you. In our playroom we have:

- Dolls and puppets that can represent family members
- Stuffed animals, cars, trucks, boats, airplanes that can represent the family at a little safer distance—"the Mommy bear" or "the Mommy truck" instead of "the Mommy"
- Play money, to help get at worries about family finances
- Doll houses and building sets, which can provide a focus for sleep problems and questions about family security
- Medical toys and real medical equipment for directed medical play

With the kinds of toys that represent your areas of concern, you can start off the playing. Say, for example: "You be the Daddy doll, walking into the doctor's office. What do you think is going to happen there?"

Just at the beginning, guide the play: "And I'll be the little girl doll, sitting at home. What does she say? What's she feeling now, do you think?"

Pretty soon the child will probably take over the little drama and direct all the characters.

Medical Play

Medical play can be especially informative. You can get doctor and nurse kits at a toy store, and a lot of hospitals will lend you the kind of equipment they'll be using in the parent's treatment.

There are two ways you can use medical equipment: for education and for directed play.

Educationally, you can demonstrate for a child exactly what's going to happen to the sick parent—a catheter here because Mom can't get up to go to the bathroom; a breathing tube in the mouth; an IV line because with the tube in her mouth, Mom won't be able to eat for a while. This is good, useful information, but it's not medical *play.*

A lot of your child's interest and anxiety right now is medical, and medical play—making up stories—can bring out what's going on in her mind. As she "treats" the Daddy doll, she'll display her understanding of what's wrong and what will be happening in the hospital. Knowing what she *thinks* is going on can help you guide her to a better understanding.

She'll also give you insights into her own medical worries. Children do worry about their own health, especially when there's serious illness in the family. Again, the play can help you to help your child to a better understanding, even if it's just repeating the mantra, "No, sweetie, there's no way the little girl doll can catch cancer from the Daddy doll."

Directed Drawing

I asked a little girl, whose father was under treatment for cancer, to draw what she would wish for if she had three wishes.

This is what she drew:

- A cigarette with the universal "no" symbol across it.
- A little girl lying in bed, dreaming of skeletons and wolves.
- A man and a woman shouting at each other.

When I showed the picture to her mother and father, they were absolutely shocked. With a single picture, their daughter had told them three things that they'd had no idea of and that they really needed to know:

- She blamed Dad's smoking habit for his cancer.
- She was having constant bad dreams.
- Their bickering was tearing her up.

Probably your younger children draw a lot of pictures without any prompting from you. And, if they're like most kids, every picture will quickly come before you with "See what I drew?" But if you want to find out what kind of pictures are going around inside your children's heads, there's one sure-fire way to start them drawing:

"How about making a picture for Daddy in the hospital?"

That lets them do something they like to do anyway and feel good about doing it.

You can also suggest the sure-fire subject: "What about making Daddy a picture of all of us?"

The way your child perceives his own family can tell you a great deal about his state of mind. It may surprise you. And it might convey some very important messages:

A six-year-old boy drew this one, and he's sending a message just as clear as Moira's.

His father has cancer and is undergoing radiation therapy. That makes Dad irritable all the time; he can't or won't control his anger. He'd been an active man, a successful businessman, who'd enjoyed teaching his son to ride a bike, spiral a football. Now he's at home, sick—and angry.

This is a picture of trouble. The little boy sees his father's face as huge, fierce, and furious—and looking right out at the child drawing it. The boy sees himself as tiny and insignificant in relationship, and he's drawn a series of lines around himself—there's a sense, almost, of waves coming at this child, waves of rage beating him down. Or those lines may be some sort of barrier to protect himself from that rage; I don't know, and it doesn't really matter.

The father's face is drawn in great detail, but the little boy hardly sees himself at all. The message here is simple, easy to read, and vital to deal with:

"Daddy's mad at me all the time."

Looking at this picture with me, the boy's mother understood that she must now take a stronger, more active role in the relationship, must try to break down the tensions that were coming between her husband and her son—*she must protect the child from that rage.*

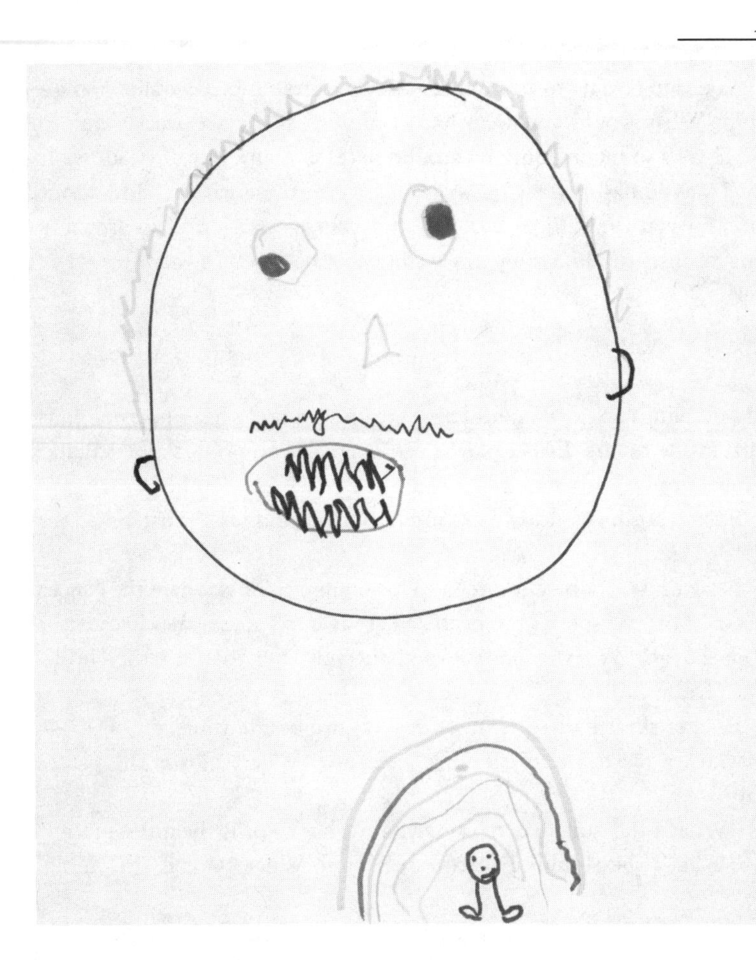

Suggesting Subjects

If you think your child is troubled, or upset, or confused about what's going on, you can direct his natural inclination to draw and gain important insights painlessly. The "Three Wishes" drawing is a nifty tool; it provides a nice, safe opportunity for your child to show you what's on his mind.

If your child wishes for a million dollars, a new bike (with speeds!), and a hundred more wishes, chances are that he or she is coping just fine. But you may also get something as revealing and insightful as that little girl's three pictures.

You don't want to get too specific, *too* directing. I wouldn't ask a child, "What would you wish for Mommy?" But it's perfectly fine to say "There's so much going on around here, so many things we all want now. I was thinking what I'd wish for if I had three wishes. How about you? Can you draw three wishes?" (Of course, your child is probably going to insist on knowing *your* wishes too; better have them ready!)

Body Drawings

Body drawings are a wonderful tool for finding out what's hurting your child, inside or out. Either parent can play; all you need is a pencil and a handful of bright crayons.

Sketch a gingerbread-man kind of outline and say: "That's me!" or "That's Daddy!"

Now draw in a bright circle: "This orange color is where the cancer is." Or "This red spot is my heart, where it hurts sometimes because of the operation." A few more colors about you, and then it's the child's turn: "Draw you!"

Let her sketch a little gingerbread figure beside yours.

"Pick a place where *you* don't feel good. What color is the place? Why?"

"What's the quiet place inside you? What color is the quiet place?"

"What's the thinking place inside you? What color is the thinking?"

That little outline can provide you with a much fuller, vividly colored insight into how your child feels and is handling the family crisis.

Directed Play and Drawing: A Caution

All of these structured activities are really good for your children—not only do they guide you, but they also give the children that indispensable sense of closeness, security, and love. So if certain things about your children's conduct concern you—anger, fear, new behaviors—you can safely direct their playing or drawing to those areas, *as long as you don't force them to confront things they're not ready to confront.*

If your five-year-old says, "I don't want to do that" or "I don't want to play that right now" or "I don't want to make a picture of witches; I want to make a picture of a police car," then back away; let her have that amount of control. As long as you, the parent, recognize that the child may be too threatened, for whatever reason, to push into certain areas, then this kind of directed play and directed drawing is both safe and enormously valuable for both of you.

"Be Happy, Mon!"

Now let's look at another picture/message:

The artist was a schoolgirl, around age eleven or twelve. Her mom had cancer, the prognosis was good, but the treatment was agonizingly long—Mom was somewhere around the middle of eighteen months of chemotherapy. It's a well-drawn picture yet oddly depersonalized; the child here appears to be another creature, separate from herself. And there's that remarkable, courageous line, in the midst of crisis:

"Don't worry; be happy, mon!"

When we talked, the girl did not want to know *anything* about her mother's medical situation. Each time I raised it with her, she would change the subject. She didn't want to visit her mother in the hospital; didn't want to see the medical unit where her mother would be cared for.

Here, the mother and I decided, is a child trying very hard to cope *and doing it pretty well.* She's trying to keep a good attitude, to stay positive. She's developed some skills of her own to maintain mental wellness. And part of how she copes is just to try to be happy, not to worry, *not to think about bad things.*

Her picture, and her attitude, told us very clearly: This girl is in a state of denial; she is refusing to face the situation, and that's how she's coping. *And right now, that's okay.*

Scarlett's Way

In a situation like this, where Mom's medical condition is going to continue and nothing will change drastically for a while—perhaps a long while—it's all right for your children to dodge the bullet, to say,

like Scarlett O'Hara, "I'm not going to think about that today. I'll think about that tomorrow."

If that denial lets your children cope, if their schoolwork keeps up, if they keep getting along with their friends, if no other signs of trouble turn up—then they are coping *successfully,* and you probably should allow them their denial.

What you do, as a parent, is make an offer: "Do you want me to tell you about Mom?" If the answer is no, that's fine, at least for now. *Don't impose information on a child who doesn't want it.* Let the child decide.

Only if the patient's situation takes a sharp turn, if life-or-death matters become imminent, should you begin to force your way past the child's barriers, to say "I know you don't want to know, but there's a problem now, and you need to be prepared." Unless or until that happens, then "Don't worry; be happy, mon!" is perfectly all right.

You might even want to try a small dose of it yourself.

It's Your Call

Remember: You, Mom, you, Dad, are the expert on your children. When you sense that something is different, something *is* different. And sometimes—often—all that's needed is to sit down and talk, and to help your son or daughter bring the doubt, the fear, the anger to the surface where you can look at it together.

There's a contradiction here. Your children need this extra time and attention just when you have less time and attention for them than ever. Here are a couple of suggestions for coping with the contradiction.

- Set aside a time—ten minutes at night, perhaps—to go over their day, to let them open up to you. Take the relaxed moments around bedtime and bathtime to chat, free-form.
- Every family has things it does together—take a bike ride, walk down to the park, toss a football. Even amid the pressure of illness, of your own doubts and concerns, set aside time to do those things. That's where your children will talk to you—verbally, and in so many other ways.

These few special moments of attention help in two ways.

- They let you spot signs of impending trouble.
- They increase your children's sense of security at the very time they need it most. The conscious investment of just a small piece of your dwindling time can pay tremendous dividends for the health and comfort of your children for years to come.

WARNING SIGNS THAT A CHILD NEEDS HELP

In the next chapter we'll talk more about what you can do, and the help you may need, to cope with signs of trouble *before* they turn into serious problems. But for now, let's look at a few specific warning flags your children may wave at you.

Early Warning #1: Sleep Disturbances

Sleep disturbances are early warnings in two senses—they can signal trouble brewing, and they are especially important in toddlers, who aren't yet verbal enough to *tell* you they're in trouble but who can *show* you.

We're not talking about the child who, in this stressful time, doesn't want to go to bed or doesn't want to sleep alone. When a youngster is lonely, scared or upset, and looking for security, it's perfectly normal to want to sleep in Mommy's bed "Just for tonight, *please?*" And, just for tonight, you may give in. Or you may compromise.

- Set up a cot for the child in your room—"Just 'til Daddy comes home, you understand?"
- Leave the child in her own room, but with her door and your door open.
- Set up a night-light.

Do what feels right to counter these normal night fears.

But when the child is living in her own house, her own room, her own bed, and with a parent at hand, then *sleep disturbance* is a serious sign; you want to deal with it without delay. If your child:

- Is continually having bad dreams
- Repeatedly wakes in the night and wanders around the house
- Repeatedly wakes from nightmares she can't quite remember
- Walks in her sleep

then that child is seriously stressed and isn't overcoming the stress in her waking hours.

SLEEP DISTURBANCES: WHAT CAN YOU DO?

Your first approach should be to help children work through the stress *while they are awake.* Give them options, verbal and physical. Set aside talk times, and help them talk through what's bothering them, the questions and uncertainties they're carrying into bed. Look at some of the conversational ideas in the next chapter, under "**How to Fish for Answers.**"

Encourage plenty of physical activity; help your children tire themselves out with a lot of play. Just using the body hard can flush out a host of mental poisons. You've probably done this yourself; you know how a fast game of racquetball can counter the mental miseries of the workplace. Kids' bodies work just like yours.

Keep your children's bedtime a calm time, focused on *them.* They shouldn't be going to bed while Mom is on the phone, talking to Grandma about how sick Daddy is. Get off the phone, get off the world, snuggle up for fifteen minutes, and read them a bedtime story with a happy ending. A story, a tuck-in, a kiss, and a cuddle can do wonders to promote a good night's sleep . . . for all of you.

Sleep Disturbances: The Danger

One vital reason to attack sleep disturbances right away is this: A child who is overtired, whose sleep is constantly disturbed, *is at great risk for other problems.* You certainly know this from your own experience: When you're overtired, even routine stresses become overwhelming. *You just can't cope.* And your overtired child will lose his ability to cope with all the other stresses—of school, of friends, of having a sick parent.

If you've done your best to handle the sleep problem just between you and your child, and the disturbance continues, is becoming chronic, *that's a sign you need outside help.*

The place to start is with the school counselor or hospital social worker, both of whom may have suggestions to alleviate the sleep disturbance. But if the troubles continue, then think about getting help from a mental health professional—a psychologist or psychiatrist. In the next chapter we'll talk about how to find the right one.

Early Warning #2: Eating Disturbances

"I Say It's Spinach, and I Say the Hell with It."

A sharp change in your child's eating patterns can be a warning sign of other troubles, particularly in a preschooler. But let's get clear what is and isn't a change in eating patterns.

Many children are picky; almost all are intolerant of new foods. Yet frequently, when someone gets sick in the family, that's exactly when Mom decides to turn over a new leaf: "All right, from now on, *this family is going to eat healthy.* We're going to have leafy vegetables four times a day, no more fat, no more cholesterol, no more________." (You fill in the blank from among the ten kinds of junk food your kids love most.)

I remember one family in which the father became ill, and the four-year-old son basically stopped eating. His mother was frantic. But when we started talking about what she was feeding him, it turned out she'd drastically altered the family menu. Suddenly, instead of the peanut butter sandwiches that had sustained him for the past year or two, there were . . . *rice cakes!* And this young man basically folded his four-year-old arms and announced, "Uh-uh. I'm not eating that. *That's not food.*"

This wasn't an eating disturbance; it was simply disturbed eating.

The fact is, with one parent seriously ill, too much has changed already in your children's lives. This is not the time to fool around with diet or any other part of the family routine that can be left alone.

Try to keep as much as possible just the way it was, because one thing—a parent's health—has changed so much.

A true eating disturbance is a change in your child's normal patterns. All children go through cycles of eating more, then eating less. But:

- If your child seems to be eating constantly, overeating, without ever getting much satisfaction from the food, or
- If the child seems to be eating very little over an extended period, picking at food, staring at it with that This-really-isn't-gonna-do-it look, avoiding mealtimes,

then you're dealing with eating disturbance, and your child's mealtime behavior is telling you something larger and deeper.

Eating problems are an indicator that your child is not handling the whole situation well. So trying to do something *about the eating* is likely to be counterproductive. Yet too often, parents who see a lot of other things spinning out of control think, "Well, this, at least, I can deal with." They turn a child's eating problem into a contest of wills, and they start to nag. Bad mistake.

The first thing to do about the problem is to *let it alone for a while.* Particularly if you're concerned with undereating, remember this: *No child is ever going to starve himself to death just because a parent is sick.*

When your son or daughter gets hungry enough, he or she will eat. So give it time; *most* children react to stress at first by undereating; some overeat. If they're handling the stress, they get past the eating problem.

An eating problem is an alert, a signal; it tells you something else is going on. That means you want to focus, not on the eating behavior, but on finding the underlying cause. In calm (non-mealtime) moments, start to ask some open-ended, "fishing" questions:

"I notice you're eating all the time, and you're never really hungry. Something on your mind? Let's talk."

Since eating problems are a frequent sign with children too young to verbalize their worries, you might get out some toys, play some "house" and medical games, then watch and listen for clues to what's on their minds.

Exercise is a good idea both for the overeater and the undereater; it will take their minds off their troubles and work up a real appetite.

Once again, the next chapter will offer more suggestions on ways to help your children—and how to find outside help if it should be needed.

Keep in mind one final point: Children's eating, like so much else about their behavior, goes in cycles as they grow. And stress can bring on the next cycle. So a change in pattern—from what you consider undereating, say, to what you consider overeating—if not accompanied by other signs of trouble, may simply be the next phase coming along ahead of time. Remain calm.

Early Warning #3: Fear

All kids—all people, for that matter—are afraid of something sometimes. It's a good thing we are; there's a lot of dangerous stuff out there, and some normal, healthy fear simply gives us the common sense to avoid it.

But now we're talking about the abnormal: fears that your children didn't have before and that won't go away.

The fear can be of almost anything, or nothing; it can be closely linked to the parent's illness or mystifyingly unrelated. I've seen:

- Fear of going to the hospital for a visit
- Fear of being left home, of *not* going to the hospital
- Fear of being with the sick parent
- Fear of *leaving* the sick parent
- Fear of a harmless neighbor
- Fear of mailmen, or people in uniform
- A constant fear without any specific form

It can be almost any kind of fear. The warning sign is that your child becomes afraid of things she wasn't afraid of before and that these new fears continue over time.

Early Warning #4: Developmental Trouble: *Failure NOT Permitted*

There is one very serious way your child will warn you of trouble: He or she will begin to fail.

A toddler who is toilet-trained suddenly isn't toilet-trained anymore. A first or second grader who was reading just fine, developing vocabulary by leaps and bounds, suddenly stops reading, stops adding new words. A daughter drops out of band practice or French club. A teen-ager loses interest in classes; As and Bs turn into Cs, Ds, and Incompletes.

Loss of skills may be your child's most urgent warning to you that something is wrong.

There's a natural tendency here, and it's a bad one—bad for you, bad for your children. It's the tendency to say "Well, no wonder! With all that's going on, of *course* Davey or Julie is failing chemistry." It's a tendency you, as the parent, must fight in yourself and must fight (and it can be a tough battle) in Davey's or Julie's teachers.

The teachers should know, of course, what's going on; to the extent you're comfortable, you should bring them into the loop. But as a parent, you must make it unmistakably clear to the teachers: You expect your child to continue to perform, and you expect the teachers to expect that too.

If there's trouble in school, meet with the teachers involved *and take your son or daughter to the meetings;* make him or her a part of what's going on. Children, especially teens, can be positively paranoid if they think something that affects them is going on behind their backs.

You won't find many absolutes in this book but here is one:

The very worst favor you can confer on your children is to allow them to fail.

Even in the presence of grave illness—even after a death—life, growth, learning, and achievement must go on. The pattern you set now will be lifelong.

Of course, it doesn't serve any purpose to *punish* the failure; that can only alienate the child, tear the two of you apart when you most need to be together, and ensure further failure. What then?

Your most sensible course is to be frank and straightforward as to what you expect. Say: "Mom and I know you're hurting. There's no way around the hurt. But what's not okay is for you to let go in school. It's Mom's job to try to get well. It's your job to keep up your grades, to keep on keeping on—to keep us as proud of you as we've always been."

Remember this for the future: A lot of children experience significant failures immediately following a loss. If those failures are not addressed right at the time they're occurring, they can lead to a *cycle* of failure that will give your child no chance to succeed—ever.

More About School

What's happening in school—beyond that central issue of success or failure—can tell you a lot about what's happening in your child. In fact,

- School problems
- Bad behavior
- School avoidance
- Fighting with schoolmates

are all clear warnings. For the school-age child they are *diagnostic* of trouble.

Again, you want to make absolutely sure your child's school knows what's going on at home. Here's an example of why the school *must* know.

One little girl was referred to me after missing three of the past four school days because of "stomach aches."

The first time, she'd persuaded the lady she was staying with, the mother of a schoolmate, that she was too ill to go; on two other days she'd reported to the school nurse with her "stomach ache," and the nurse had simply sent her home. What the nurse didn't know, and should have been told, was that the little girl's father was undergoing a bone marrow transplant at a hospital four or five hours from home. Understandably, he wanted his wife with him during the frightening procedure and the recovery period—a total of four weeks. So the child was sent to stay with a friend. She wasn't happy about it but seemed to accept it. But as soon as Mom went away, the little girl fell apart.

And it had happened once before. Weeks earlier, when the father went in to prepare for his bone marrow harvest, the little girl had gotten so sick that the parents had to rush straight home. The next morning they drove all the way back to the hospital; Dad was overtired and edgy—a bad way to undergo a surgical procedure.

The little girl's stomach aches were real—*the stomach aches are always real.* But they had nothing to do with a bug, or a virus, or eating something or not eating something else.

So we sent Mom home, all those hours over the road, to spend some time with the little girl, to talk to the friend's mother, and to explain the matter at school. I believed the little girl *could* handle the separation, but she needed a lot more support than she'd been getting so far. No one had really talked to her. And I suspect that, somewhere below the level of consciousness, she thought, if she just got sick enough, Mom would come home.

School avoidance behavior is most likely in kids who are already struggling in school or having problems there. In fact, if your child is a really good student and starts having some school troubles, you might let that go on a little longer than if he's a marginal student.

The good student will probably snap back; school is, after all, a pleasure and an escape from the problems at home. But the marginal student is more likely to say "This is a miserable time in my life anyway, and school just makes me more miserable, makes me feel crummy inside." In a way, he's taking advantage—finding an excuse not to do what he doesn't want to do anyway—but it's not a conscious scheme. It's just another expression of misery.

Yet even the good student, faced with a family medical calamity, may need "permission" to enjoy school. I'm thinking of three children I saw recently: a girl fifteen, a boy eleven, and a girl nine. Their father had suffered a massive heart attack. He'd been put on a heart-mate, an electrical pump, to keep him alive until a donor heart could be found for transplant.

All three kids were really good students and involved in all kinds of extracurricular activities—soccer, gymnastics, modern dance, peewee football. Their mom and I talked to them about what was going on and how they'd be going to stay for a while with an aunt they liked. And I told them something to the effect that "Your part now is to get back to school, to do as good a job as you possibly can with your regular life and activities, and to let your mom stay at the hospital so she can give your dad the support he needs."

They were absolutely astonished. And they asked me, "You mean, it's *okay* to go back to school? It's *okay* to do the things we like to do?"

They went back the next day. Their father remains critically ill, but they needed to get back to their normal life *because that life is their support.* And first they needed permission to return to it—just as, sometimes, in the midst of all that's happening, *your* children may need permission to laugh, to play, to have fun.

And you have to tell them, that's okay.

School: The Up Side

There's a good-news side to this story: If your child is continuing to do well *in school,* then he's probably okay, no matter what bad things you may be seeing *at home.*

In fact, you may be seeing your kids at their worst, what with "You don't pay any attention to me anymore," and "Why can't my friends come over for a rock party tonight?" and the third time their room-door slams hard enough to rattle the walls.

Remember this: If your kids can put together six consecutive hours each day during which they're coping, interacting with friends, and getting their work done, *then they're probably okay,* no matter what kind of troublesome behavior you may be seeing at home.

Early Warning #5: Beware the Quiet Child

Remember Moira? Moira, I said, was easy. Moira was *quiet.*

More even than the child who screams, breaks things, and gets into fights, I worry about the quiet child. And the reason is, for parents distracted by illness or worse, that child *is* easy—easy to ignore. Stressed parents tend to accept gratefully when a child sort of disappears into the wallpaper. But when a child who used to be lively, noisy, even troublesome—in a word, normal—suddenly retreats into silence, that child is silently warning you of trouble to come.

If your son or daughter responds to the family crisis by going silent—by "going away"—you should go after him or her. Find time to talk or play together, and try to draw out what's going on. Say: "I notice you get kind of quiet when you're worried. Are you worried now?"

You might present some of the possible causes and see how your child responds:

"Are you thinking a lot about Dad?"

"Are some of your pals kind of insensitive?"

"Are you worried about going off to camp—about what might happen while you're there?"

"Are you having trouble keeping up in school, with all that's going on around here?"

You may not get a response the first time you ask, or the fifth time. Kids are like that. But keep reaching out, keep following your quiet child into the silence.

The Little Girl Who Didn't Care

A young father brought his five-year-old to our Program. His wife was in the hospital recuperating from a heart transplant. She was not doing well. And their daughter, Sara, didn't seem to care.

"She's acting as if her mother doesn't even exist," he said. "She won't talk about it, won't listen when I tell her how Mom's doing. I don't know whether she's happy or sad; *she just won't address it!*"

At her kindergarten, the little girl was acting hyper—starting fights, beginning a typical downhill spiral toward the unpleasant label of "troublemaker."

Sara and I decided it might be nice to make an audiotape for her mom. Sara sang a little song, then, as I reached for the switch, she said, "Don't turn it off." And Sara started to talk about cooking—about making chicken. Then she said, sadly, "Grandma was a good cooker."

Sara's father had told me that his mother had died a few months earlier—and that, with the sudden onset of his wife's grave illness, he hadn't even had time to think about his mother's death; he couldn't even grieve. He'd "put it on hold." He'd never talked to Sara about her grandmother's death.

Now I said to Sara, "Your daddy is sad about Grandma." And she said, "You know who else is sad? Me."

With the tape running, Sara told me about her grandmother; she'd lived in her own apartment and every day Sara would go over to help her.

I said, "Gee, it sounds like you helped her a lot."

"Yeah," the little girl said miserably, "*until she died.*"

And then it came out: "She wouldn't have died if I had helped her more." This child believed that she hadn't helped her grandmother enough to save her. It's the most dramatic example I've encountered of a young child's "magical thinking"—what happens around me happens because of me, and I have the Power: If something goes wrong, it means I did something wrong.

Sara couldn't *begin* to cope with her mother's illness, because she had never gotten through her grandmother's death. It was all right—it was normal—for her *father* to say, "I'll grieve about my mother later, after we get through this new thing," but Sara couldn't handle it that way.

So at last they cried together about Grandma, and then they cried together about Mom.

Only after they talked about Grandma—after Dad and I had reassured Sara that her help and love were the very best thing in his mother's last days and that she had told him so—only then could Sara get past that earlier tragedy and begin to deal with her mother's illness. And within a few days Sara began to ask the normal questions about her mother: Where is Mommy's old heart? Why isn't the new one working right? At school, she was the old, cheerful Sara.

Because we all like happy endings and are entitled to know about them, I'll tell you that after one terrible month, Sara's mother and her new heart decided to get along together; she wound up with an amazingly good outcome to the transplant.

Remember, as you begin to cope with this new family crisis: If your children have any unresolved *earlier* crises going around in their heads—the recent loss of a pet, a serious school problem, encounters with abuse or crime, a recent divorce—*they'll have to deal with the earlier crisis before they can handle a new one.* If they're still sad or upset about it, if they haven't talked it through, if it's still churning inside, unresolved, then when something new comes along, *they may simply shut down.* Their capacity to cope is overloaded. And before you can help them through the present, you're going to have to help them through the past.

The Warning Signs of Suicide

Up to now, we've been dealing mostly with mental, psychological, and emotional damage to children. But, in fact, children are young human beings and are capable of almost everything their elders are capable of—including, intentionally or not, hurting themselves.

Some studies in the past few years suggest that children, even very young children, *even children too young to understand what death is,* may attempt to hurt or kill themselves. Luckily very few young children succeed, but there is some evidence that teen-agers who do, tragically, manage to take their own lives may have made earlier, unsuccessful tries when considerably younger.

The Three Levels of Danger

Generally, in the area of real, physical dangers, we see children operating at three levels—of increasing seriousness and, fortunately, of decreasing frequency. But let's be clear on one thing: *Every one of these levels of talk or action is to be taken very seriously indeed; the question is not whether to pay attention, but what to do.* The three levels are:

1. **Talking about it**
2. **Taking risks**
3. **The real thing**

Talking About It

In this fiber-optic age, in our hardwired society, there's hardly a child of six who hasn't heard about suicide or who doesn't have *some* idea of what it means. And your children will talk about it. Sometimes it will be perfectly meaningless: "I'm flunking geometry; oh, God, I think I'll kill myself!" "My boyfriend dumped me; there's nothing to live for."

But in your current family crisis, this kind of talk can be a real cry of despair and a plea for help. If your child is obviously depressed by what's going on around him, and you begin to hear "I wish I wasn't alive," or "I just don't want to live any more," *it is always serious.* That doesn't mean that the next day your child will actually make an attempt, but he's playing around with the big issues of what life is and how one handles emotional pain: ultimate questions of being and not-being.

How Do I Deal with This?

First, *you never ignore it; you never ridicule it; you never deny children their feelings.* If the words are there, the thought is somewhere, and *attention must be paid.*

By now I hope you're coming to share my belief that communication is the key to almost everything between parent and child in times of stress; that the parent's job is to keep doors open and keep opening doors. So when your child tells you through tears, "I wish I could die, so I'd never have to hear you and Mommy fighting any more," you must *never* say what for many parents is the most natural thing in the world to say: *"That's the most ridiculous thing I ever heard; I don't ever want to hear you say anything like that again."* Because you may get your wish; you may never hear your child say it again. But the thought behind the words is still there, festering deep inside—and you've just cut off the chance of bringing it out into daylight, looking it over, and dealing with it.

What you do is pretty simple. First, you pay full attention. Then you try to find out how serious the child may be: Is he just thinking about it? Or has he crossed the line to thinking about *how* to do it?

An unfocused, unhappy "I wish I were dead" is probably something you can deal with, talk out. But if you discover that your child has begun to think about particular methods of hurting or killing himself, that is an absolute indication that *you need immediate, professional help, on the level of a psychiatrist or a psychologist.*

THE QUESTIONS TO ASK

The kinds of questions you'll want to ask are open-ended, putting the ball in the child's court. Avoid questions that can be answered with a shrug or a nod, a yes or a no.

You might start along these lines: "You seem really sad these days. Tell me what you're feeling inside . . . tell me what kinds of things you're thinking about."

If the child says something like: "I don't think I want to live anymore," "Nothing's fun anymore," or "Nothing's ever going to be the same again," then you can continue probing, with more nonthreatening, open-ended questions:

"What does that mean? What do you think you might do? Are there things you can think of that would make your life happier again?"

I can't script these conversations; each answer determines the next question. The important thing is *not to put ideas into children's heads,* not to ask specific, will-you-or-won't-you questions, but to help the child explore what's going on and how he might become happier.

The issue is most likely to arise with older school-age children or teen-agers; they're old enough to understand the concept of death, and they've been exposed to the idea of suicide in school, on television, and probably in their own conversations. And because they have that sophistication, I think it *is* safe for parents to address the issue directly.

When a child says, sadly, "I just feel like killing myself," it's perfectly appropriate for you to take that head-on, to say "Gosh, it really makes me sad to hear you say that. Tell me what you're thinking about. Tell me if you're thinking about how you might do that. Tell me if your friends have been talking about that. If you were going to do something like that, tell me what you might actually do."

Boys and Girls Are Different

There really aren't a whole lot of behavioral differences between preschool boys and preschool girls. But once they reach school age, they begin to diverge, and the parent has to think about them differently. Somebody once said that "All girls are born actresses, but very few boys are born actors." True or not, I find that school-age and teen-age girls are the ultimate dramatists. And what they dramatize most is themselves; they are constantly the stars of their own TV shows. Your daughter who decides at thirteen "I'll never have a boyfriend; I'll just kill myself" probably will have a boyfriend, and probably won't kill herself.

But *a suicide statement from a boy should probably be taken more seriously than the same statement from his sister.* Because boys don't self-dramatize to the extent that girls do, because they tend to keep bad stuff inside them, boys are more serious when they talk about suicide. It's very hard indeed for a boy to surface a comment like that, and it indicates a deep anguish within.

Handling It—Continued

If your child hasn't gone beyond that generalized "I'm just so sad, I wish I could end all this," you can probably deal with it. And one way to do that is by laying out alternatives.

Your child can build up that terrific load of pain. But children are also better than adults at seeing options—they tend to be more optimistic than grown-ups; more of the stories they tell have happy endings.

Remind your child that this illness isn't forever. Talk about specific good times coming and what you'll do then—on the next birthday, or Saturday at Great Adventure, or next spring when school's out, or Friday night when we play Westwood High. Again, physical activity, from punching the heavy bag to riding a bike to taking karate lessons, is a good way to boil off the emotional poisons. If you can find a way, get out and do something together that's fun.

Manipulation

And keep in mind: Kids, especially kids in those middle years from about eight to eleven, are the most incredible manipulators. If they see that "I just think I'll kill myself" gets a rise out of you every time they say it, then they'll keep saying it for all it's worth.

The key to heading off that kind of manipulation is your own expert knowledge of your children. You make mood judgments all the time. If the child doesn't look terribly "down," if there's that certain glint in the eye that says "put-on," if she's sort of watching your reaction out of the corner of an eye when she says "I just think I'll kill myself," then something *other* than a real suicide threat is going on.

And a child who is really sad, really depressed, doesn't bounce back right away. So your son, who says "I just think I'll kill myself" and a few minutes later is outside playing with his best friend, isn't telling you something serious about self-destruction. Nevertheless, *he is telling you something serious.*

These little manipulations aren't conscious on your child's part. And they *are* a cry for help. They're an attempt to gain your time and your attention, and that's what the child is telling you he needs: your time and your attention; your feedback, your approval—the normal, accustomed parent/child things that may be overwhelmed by the family crisis. So even when a suicide threat is not a suicide threat, attention must be paid; it *is* always an early warning of trouble.

Making It Better

One thing a parent can do immediately is help the child come up with things to make him or her feel better, more positive. Ask your child, "Would you like to feel better? Can you and I together find ways to make you feel better? What can we do together?"

Remember, a child's nature is basically optimistic. So if you can open a door toward feeling better, your child will walk through it.

One tactic I've found effective is to focus on something, just one thing, that's been good in a terrible day.

"Hon, I've had a rotten day too. But I did have one fun thing: Coming home from the store, I met this *beautiful* Old English sheepdog. And what do you think his name was? Heathcliffe! Can you imagine? Can you think of just one really good thing that happened to you this rotten day?"

"Affect": A Key Indicator

Here I'd like to raise the idea of "affect." It's a term we use to describe the way the child *appears* to you or to me: If your son or daughter is constantly "down"—in chronic distress, in continuing emotional pain, just doesn't "lift" very often; if the things that always used to bring pleasure no longer bring pleasure—*then you definitely need outside help.*

Risky Business

This child is past the talking stage. This child is *doing.* What he or she is doing is taking risks:

- Darting out from between cars into traffic
- Balancing on the railing of a bridge
- Teetering along the narrow top of a high wall

The actions bring your heart into your mouth; they make you want to grab the child and shake or slap the stupidity out of him. It may not be actual suicidal behavior, but it is the child pushing the envelope, seeing just how far he can go and still pull back to safety.

These actions actually are a huge, silent cry for help: "Please pay attention to me. I can't stand this. I'm on the edge; you've got to do something to help me."

Once you understand that—once you understand that the high-risk behavior, the car-dodging, edge-walking, pill-tasting is a cry for help—then you understand that *the help your child needs now is professional.* You're past the point where you can *risk* tackling the problem yourself, past the point where such first-resource people as school counselors and clergy can help. You can't take *any* risk.

When you see your child in overt acts that threaten his physical well-being or his life, it's time to bring in a psychologist or a psychiatrist.

The Real Thing

True suicide attempts by children are the rarest of all; you'll probably never deal with them. Yet they do happen—a child will cut her wrists, swallow a vial of pills, climb to the top of a bridge *with the serious intention of dying.*

Once again, in this most unlikely but most dangerous situation, the answer is *immediate* intervention by a psychiatrist or a psychologist, with no steps in between. A child who gets this far may well need to be hospitalized, to make absolutely sure there are no further attempts.

Throughout this chapter we've looked for trouble, and maybe we've found it. So in the next chapter let's talk about where and how to get help.

EARLY WARNINGS: A SUMMARY

We *won't* worry about the occasional bad day

We *will* worry about continuing patterns: behavior problems that don't go away (page 47)

The goal: to identify and change stress reactions *before* they do damage (page 47)

Some things you may be seeing or hearing:

- Fear and anxiety (page 48)
- Toys that vanish (page 48)
- Aggressive play (page 48)

Some ways you can direct children's play, and interpret it:

- Getting the atmosphere right (page 49)
- Some toys that can help you get information (page 49)
- What you should say and do (page 49)
- Medical play: it can tell you a lot (page 50)

Some ways you can direct their drawing:

- Understanding what they draw: some examples (page 50)
- Subjects you can suggest (page 52)

A *caution:* don't force the play or drawing if your children are reluctant (page 54)

Making time for your kids when you don't have time:

- Bedtime and bath-time (page 57)
- Try to keep doing the "family things" you all do together (page 57)
- Two benefits of making time: helping you and helping them (page 57)

Here are some important *warning signs* that a child needs help:

- Major changes or disturbance in *sleep* (page 58)
- Major changes or disturbance in *eating* (page 60)
- Appearance of *fears* that weren't there before (page 61)
- Developmental trouble: loss of skills, falling grades (page 62)

  Remember: the very worst favor you can confer on your children now is to allow them to fail.
- The quiet child (page 66)

The warning signs of suicide (page 68)

Three levels of danger, and what you should do (page 68)

REMEMBER: You are the expert on your children. When you sense that something is different, or something is wrong, *you're probably right.*

FOUR

Help! How to Give It, Where to Get It

RIPPLES

Something in the last chapter has registered; a sign of trouble has clicked with you. You think your child is giving a signal and, because you're the mom or dad, you're probably right.

We're going to look at help as a widening set of ripples, starting right in the center with you and your children and working outward through the circles of help available as the problem proves increasingly tough.

The good news is, you probably won't have to go very far out from the center: you and your kids together. Most of the time, parents tell me, forewarned *is* forearmed. When they know what problems to expect, and how to react, the little troubles don't turn into big troubles; Mom and Dad find they can get on top of the issues, get past them, and help their children get on with their lives. In about half my practice, I never even see the children; the parents themselves can handle the problems. And I'm about the third ripple.

"I KNOW WORSE WORDS!"

Her name was Joanie. She was about seven years old, and she had a brain tumor. Because she'd been having chemotherapy, her eating was disrupted; for a while she lost everything she ate. But now the treatment was over; she should have been recovering. Nevertheless, Joanie still wouldn't eat, not even her very favorite food, graham crackers. And the doctors couldn't release her from the hospital until she started taking real food. Could I see her?

What I saw, tiny in the middle of a pediatric bed, was a bald, skinny, pale, depressed, just miserable little kid. She wouldn't really talk to me; she certainly wouldn't smile.

I persuaded Joanie to go to the playroom with me and trundled her off through the hospital corridors in a wheelchair. In the playroom, the one thing—the only thing—Joanie would do was to draw; Joanie loved to make pictures.

She started to draw a dinosaur. And she began folding the paper, a sort of origami thing she'd learned in kindergarten, to make the dinosaur three dimensional. We talked as she worked, and, just to lighten things, I asked what we might do to make him look "really weird." She thought about that as she drew in the face. Then Joanie said, "There. I think it's done. Except . . . *do you want me to make snot dripping out of its nose?*"

I was astonished. Picture this tiny, skinny, sick, depressed, pale kid, looking at you out of enormous eyes and asking, most seriously, "Do you want me to make snot dripping out of its nose?"

Well, I cracked up. I started rocking back and forth with laughter, so Joanie started to laugh. She laughed, and laughed, and laughed.

I said, "Joanie, I can't believe you're using words like that!"

And Joanie grinned and said, *"I know worse words!"*

"You do, huh? Well, why don't you tell me some of the worst words you know?"

And she did. Most of them were kid words like poop and pee, but she had a few more advanced ones too. I just laughed and laughed through this proud litany, and so did Joanie. She wore herself out laughing.

As I rolled her back through the hospital lobby, Joanie started to review some of her words, and pretty loudly. I said, "Joanie, you can't use words like those in public!"

"Ya mean like *POOP*?" Joanie shrieked at the top of her lungs, as all eyes turned toward us. "Ya mean like *PEE*?"

When we got back to the room, the first thing Joanie asked for was a graham cracker. That afternoon the doctors sent her home. One of them told me, "If she's eating graham crackers and acting happy, there's no reason to keep her here."

Sometimes, just as the *Reader's Digest* says, laughter *is* the best medicine. And sometimes tears are. What we're going to learn to do now is to help your child reach inside to the laughter, or the tears—to the best medicine.

Getting Physical

As we work our way through your children's problems and the ripples of help available, a lot of our emphasis will be about *talking* with your kids. But let's start with a little context—what to *do* while you're talking or while you're not talking. And this advice applies no matter how much or how little help your children need.

Think for a moment about your own style and your family's style. What do you *normally* do to support your child when he's stressed? A pat on the shoulder? A hug? A snuggle? A tickle? Group hug? All these and more? Right now your whole family is stressed, and you may have a tendency to withdraw, to be at arm's length from your kids. You may not think about getting physical. But in order to support and comfort your children, you've got to give them *at least* the warmth and attention—the physical love—they've grown up with until now.

So if in the middle of some of the conversations I'll be describing, you suddenly think, "You know, a hug might be good right here," then you're certainly right.

Count on it.

The Center of the Circle of Help: You and Your Kids

How to Fish for Answers

You think your child is worried, and the worries aren't coming out. She's not asking the questions you know are inside there—about how serious your illness really is, and will we be able to see you in the hospital, and who'll take care of us, and *could you die?* And what you want to do now is get these questions on the table, so you can look at them together, get them settled, and get on with things.

What you can do is to ask some open-ended, "fishing" questions—questions that *don't* answer themselves.

For instance, the kind of question I would *never* ask a child is: "Are you afraid Mom's going to die, yes or no?" Give a child a worst-case scenario, and she'll grab it every time. The question is there, waiting within the child, but *she* has to bring it out, as part of a range of possibilities. So you might start this way:

"What kind of questions do you have?" That's open-ended, but it requires an answer. Or "You seem a little blue—what kind of feelings are you having about this?" Or "Are you feeling a little scared? What kinds of things are you afraid of?" Or "What do you think could happen?"

"What do you think will probably happen?"

"What's the best thing that could happen, do you think?"

"What's the worst thing that could happen?"

The idea is to put the ball in your child's court. Not to *make* her think, because, I promise you, deep inside she's already thinking, furiously. But to bring *her* ideas, hopes, and fears up to the surface where you can both examine them in healthy daylight. These open, non-directed questions are the way to probe *safely.*

Going Deeper

If you want to go deeper, because some specific behavior change is warning you of trouble, then focus your questions on the change itself, *not* what you think might be causing it:

"Hon, you say nothing's worrying you, but: I see you fighting a lot with your friends. . . .

"You're just not sleeping very well; I think there's something on your mind . . .

"You're very quiet, and that's not like you; usually we can't shut you up. . . .

"Now, you're the expert on you—why do you think you're doing that?"

Whatever the problem behavior is, try to question the *behavior;* let the child come up with what's behind it.

SMORGASBORD

Sometimes I'll offer a child some possibilities about what might be going on. I might say:

"A lot of kids ask me, 'Why does Dad have to go visit Mom every single night after work; why can't he stay home with us?' "

Or "A lot of kids worry about what's going to happen to Dad with Mom so sick; is that on your mind?"

Or "One kid worried that he'd have to quit basketball, because Mom can't drive him to practice."

Or "Kids ask me whether they'll still get their allowance, with Dad away."

What I'm trying to do is lay out a smorgasbord of the things kids might worry about, from the fairly trivial to the pretty serious, and let them pick. You can adapt the smorgasbord technique:

"I've read where lots of kids whose parents get sick worry that . . ." and offer some likely possibilities.

If you persist, and pick the moments when your kids are open to you, they'll usually let you into their heads and talk out what's troubling them. But if not, and the troubling behavior continues, you can begin suggesting the next level:

"I understand you don't want to talk to me about it—maybe you're not even sure yourself what's bothering you. So I'd like to find someone else you can talk to."

Getting the Emotions Out

We Americans tend to treasure a Norman Rockwell view of childhood—sunlight and porch swings and no conflict worse than a schoolyard shiner. The fact is, children are not puppies; they are not warm and cuddly. They are small human beings, confused and conflicted and in need.

In a family medical crisis, your children inevitably are going to lose some measure of parenting—and children respond very strongly to that particular loss. We can minimize the loss, but we can't make it not exist. So your pleasant, comfortable children may become angry, sullen, afraid, even mean. It's hard for you to accept; you don't want your children to display such ugly, negative emotions. Yet your job now is to let children know that the anger and the fear are okay, are *right*—and to help them live and thrive beyond those emotions.

Consciously, deliberately encourage your children to be themselves, to be children. It's okay to show emotion, it's okay to cry, and it's okay to laugh. And it's okay sometimes to get angry, to slam a door, to kick a garbage can—even to scream at you. What's not okay is to keep stuff inside that needs to get outside.

One fourteen-year-old told me that when things get just too hard to bear, she slams her bedroom door a few times. "My parents used to yell at me, but now they know I *need* to do it."

She carefully took down all the pictures on the door-side of her bedroom, so they won't get broken when it's time for a few therapeutic slams. We've even talked about slam calibration—what's a two-slam problem, compared to a four-slam problem?

Ways to Let Go

Slams or not, every child needs some private place in the house to retreat and let go—prominent in our own playroom is a big punching bag, heavily scarred from all the childhood aggressions that have been taken out on its tough hide. Punching bags, store-bought or homemade, are good; so are toys kids can kick—anything that lets them get their feelings out without having to talk about them. Sometimes we suggest the kids draw pictures of people or things they're really mad at and paste them on the punching bag—a little like Murphy Brown's dartboard. Physicality is important with kids, who can't always express themselves in words.

When you see your child tightening up, send him out for a walk or a run or a bike ride, something to divert his attention and tire him out physically. One family I know used to tear up the Yellow Pages together; they wound up with a lot of yellow paper on the floor, but in much better mental shape, and nothing got broken.

A lot of kids who seem out of control can really benefit from things like karate or *tae kwon do*—sports that emphasize control, not wildness. This focus on action is especially important for boys, who at any given age tend to be far more physical and far less verbal than girls of the same age. Some girls go after our playroom punching bag, but it's the boys who really make its life miserable.

The Sound of Pumpkins

As of last Hallowe'en, I can offer one more coping mechanism, from personal experience. There's only one problem: It's seasonal.

I'd had a really rotten week—so bad that I almost didn't answer the phone as I was leaving the office Friday night. The call was from the mother of a family that I'd worked with and liked, and the news was terrible.

The young father had just had a new MRI scan: His cancer had returned.

After all the personal and family pain of the first siege, the doctors now wanted him to return Monday to begin a whole new course of chemotherapy.

The parents told the children—a boy twelve, a girl three. All four were devastated . . . and furious. It was so unfair!

The mother told me: "We're just so angry! It wasn't supposed to be like this. . . ." And it was worse for the children—the little girl in tears; the boy shouting "I'm not going to go through this again!"

In a way it was even worse than the first time—not just because they'd hoped it was over, but because this time all four knew just how rough the next few weeks and months were going to be. Finally the mother said helplessly, "Kathleen, I think we all need to pound on something!"

I said, "Why don't you find something, and do that?" It wasn't much, but it was the only help I could offer.

On Saturday afternoon, my phone rang at home. It was the mother, very excited. She said, "We found it!"

"Found what?"

"You know the jack-o-lanterns? Do you know what it's like to hit a pumpkin with a baseball bat? *It's wonderful!*"

Late the night before, she told me, the four of them had picked up a couple of bats, gone outside, and smashed jack-o-lanterns together. They wound up with an enormous mess—and rolling with laughter.

I thought about that for a while, thought of the kind of week I'd been having. Then I dug out a bat and went outside to talk things over with my own jack-o-lantern.

It really *is* wonderful.

Helping with Relaxation and Imagery

Relaxation techniques are a good way to reduce stress, both for children and adults. Your public library has excellent books and tapes that go into as much detail as you wish.

These techniques are based on one simple principle: Stress and relaxation are incompatible. *You can't be really stressed and really relaxed at the same time.* And we *can* learn how to relax. As we make ourselves relax, the stress correspondingly disappears. Unlike love and marriage in the song, you can't have one *with* the other.

It does little good to tell your child "Don't be scared." Or "We don't want you to worry." It's a lot more helpful to tell the child *what to do* to make himself feel better. And while some kids think self-relaxation is stupid, most become really good at it. They come to love the feeling they get inside when their bodies go limp, loose, comfortable, *relaxed.*

There are all kinds of relaxation techniques. Let me describe one of them: progressive relaxation.

Make a fist. Clench it as tight as you possibly can. Now, feel how it feels—not just in your clenched fingers, but in your wrist, the back of your hand, the inside of your forearm, all the way up to your shoulder.

Got it? Now relax the fist. Feel how loose all those same muscles are. *Learn the difference* between how the muscles feel in a clenched fist and a relaxed hand. And whenever you're feeling stressed or tense, *make those muscles feel relaxed.*

If you're a child and pretty good at it, then the next time you feel like yelling at Mom, you can check: Is my arm tense? Are the muscles all stiff, like when I clench my fist? If they are, then make them relax, make them feel all loose and comfortable. That will help *you* relax, put you back in control. You'll be able to negotiate with Mom about what you want, without getting into a big fight and being sent to your room.

IMAGERY

Relaxation imagery is another step that can really help, especially with young children. Say something like this: "Close your eyes and be at the seashore—listen to the waves—feel them bubble over your ankles."

It's a way of using the mind to recapture pleasant sensations, to slow the breathing, and lower the heart rate, to *relax* and drive away stress.

Children's imagery tends to be a little more active than grown-ups'. You or I might remember lying on a beach, basking; your child is more likely to board Aladdin's flying carpet, go swooping up to the clouds, then down under the Golden Gate. It's not as passive, but it's just as relaxing.

There are self-teaching books and tapes on deep relaxation; many parents get very good at it, both with their children and with themselves.

Music

For older children there's music. A lot of teen-agers tell me they use music to get through or get around their troubles. I remember one fifteen-year-old girl in particular. Her father was awaiting a transplant, and the continuing fear and suspense were devastating. She told me: "I put on my headphones, and play the music *I* want to hear, however loud I want to play it. I let the music go right through my brain, from one side to the other."

The music going through her brain blocked everything out for her, *including her thoughts.* When this girl doesn't want to think about what's going on—and she's entitled *not* to think about it sometimes—her music lets her not think. It's a very strong technique for older kids. So if your kids love music—any kind of music, whether you can stand it or not—encourage them. Probably you should try to steer them away from gangster rap, but let them listen to whatever works.

Laughter: The Best Medicine—Sometimes

I know a family whose oldest member lives in a senior citizens' residence. One afternoon several years ago, her grandchildren came to visit. They were walking with her down the corridor toward the dining room, when an elderly gentleman passed them in the opposite direction.

Both old folks were a bit hard of hearing. So when the gentleman called out, in a friendly fashion, "Hello—are you going to lunch?" the grandmother smiled, waved, and called back cheerily, "No—I'm going to lunch!"

It's been a sure laugh line in that family ever since; any time somebody mis-hears something or gets confused, one of the kids will pipe up, "Are you going to lunch?" and the other will call back, "No, I'm going to lunch!" Then everybody dissolves.

That kind of family in-joke is a sure tension-reliever at tough moments, and the really neat part is that nobody outside the family will have the slightest idea of what you're all laughing at.

You and the kids can cheer each other up with riddles, with jokes (including those dreadful knock-knock ones)—with anything that will break through the tension.

But remember: What you don't want to do is make jokes about your children's honest concerns.

When a child is being serious, stay serious.

When your children need information or need to share a feeling with you, you never want to belittle that or pretend it isn't serious. It's when the *child* tries to lighten up, tries to say something funny, that you've got your signal: Now she's ready to break the tension.

A lot of my work involves cancer, and a lot of times I have to warn kids that their good-looking mom or dad is going to lose all her or his hair, temporarily. And it's upsetting, so I say, "It's going to be hard to see Dad without his hair, isn't it?" And the child will usually nod gloomily, and we'll talk about ways to help—maybe going out with Mom to buy Dad a couple of hats.

But usually, in a little while, I can see the child lightening up. I may ask, "How do you think your dad will look without hair?" And the child will come up with something like "I think he'll look kinda like a big hard-boiled egg!" And we'll both start to laugh.

And now you can build on that, get silly; you can suggest, "How about drawing pictures on Dad's head?" and think of what pictures might be appropriate.

And this is the pattern: Being honest with your children means exposing them to a series of new, frequently unpleasant realities. They're not going to like that, and you must respect their distress. But soon you will see them trying to find a way to cope, and that's where you can bring in humor to help them cope.

"Are you going to lunch?"

"No, I'm going to lunch!"

The Terrible, Horrible, No-Good, Very Bad Day

That's the title of one of my favorite books: *Alexander and the Terrible, Horrible, No-Good, Very Bad Day* (by Judith Viorst; New York: Macmillan Children's Book Group, 1989). I like it because I have those days, and so do you, and so do your kids. (Most of the pages end with "I think I'll move to Australia.")

They are days when, from morning to night, nothing goes right, nothing can go right, nothing will ever go right again, and even the things that do go right go wrong.

When your child is having one of those, he will absolutely defy your very finest efforts at parenting: You are *not* going to make me feel better. Try all you like, you are *not* going to help me. I can't find my favorite tennis shoe; this shirt has a spot on it and I want to *wear* it today; oh, God, did you buy skim milk again?

When those days come, for you or your child, just remember: *You can't fix it, so just let it happen.* Minimize anything that needs to be done that day. If you have plans you can postpone, postpone them. Get through the day, get everyone to bed at the end of it, and remember, if you can:

Tomorrow will be better.

Probably.

When Enough Is Enough: Talking Tough

There's a technical word in psychology: *Perseverate.* I like it because it sounds a little quirky and because there's no other word exactly like it. Perseverating is a kind of circular thinking, or maybe a downward spiral.

You begin to worry about a problem, and that makes you think how serious the problem is, and that makes you worry *a lot* more, and that makes you think how *terribly* serious it is and . . .

And you're perseverating. It's pathological—worrying at the same problem again and again without affecting the problem at all. It's something kids do a lot, especially in a family crisis. And sometimes when they do, it takes a verbal parental whack to snap them out of it.

Because you're a good parent, you want to solve every problem for your children. Maybe, secretly, you think you *should* solve every problem for them. But there are problems you can't solve. *Sometimes you can't make it better.*

So when your child comes at you, again and again, with the same unanswerable questions ("*When* is Mom going to be better?" "*Why* did you get a brain tumor?" "I'm so sad; *why* can't I go over to Sammy's and play Nintendo?"), when the child is becoming a total pest on one subject, you're dealing with perseveration.

Sometimes you can compromise, offer alternatives, break into the cycle. If the house rule is no friends until homework is finished, and Dad is at home sick, perhaps you can modify the rule a couple of afternoons a week.

But if you've done all the compromising you reasonably can, and your son or daughter still keeps coming at you with the same refrain, then it's perfectly okay to say "Look, this is the situation. I don't like it. You don't like it. *But I can't fix it.* And we're both going to have to live with it for a while. Now, knock it off!"

In the words of the old song: "I told ya I love ya; now get out!"

The First Ripple of Help: Family and Friends

Maybe it's not working. Maybe you're doing your level best, but you're just not getting anywhere. The warning signs—continuing patterns of troubling, abnormal behavior—keep flaring. Maybe the "fishing" expeditions I've described sound great in a book, but with your kids they produce only more tension and aggravation. Maybe your suggestions for helping them cope meet nothing but resentment and resistance. Maybe you and your kids are simply *too* close, or not quite close enough.

A Question of Gender

Brace yourself: Maybe there's a gender problem. Particularly with young teens, it's often terribly difficult talking about certain matters with the opposite sex—even parents. Right now one parent—one gender—is out of action. So a teen-age daughter may really need to talk out Mom's mastectomy—but she simply can't do it with Dad. A son may be horribly threatened and conflicted by Dad's testicular cancer—but it's not the kind of thing you can talk to Mom about. With teenagers, where there's a sexual component to the situation, start looking around for someone of the same sex for them to talk to. Aunts and uncles are a great resource here; grandparents can be a little too inhibiting—and inhibited. The great thing about an aunt or an uncle is that she or he is the same generation as Mom or Dad—it's like talking intimate stuff with Mom or Dad, only once removed.

And maybe *you're* too stressed. You're entitled—don't beat yourself up about it. It's perfectly okay—maybe even a little courageous—to look inside yourself and decide that you simply don't have the energy, the strength, or the time to handle this right now.

If that's the case, start talking to your kids about where *they'd* like to turn for help.

Children know which adults they're comfortable talking to—*they'll tell you if you ask them.* The answers may surprise you; they can range from an uncle you didn't think they liked very much to a teacher they hardly mention, to the mother of a not especially close friend—or they may indicate exactly the people you'd have guessed.

In one family, the five children named five different people they'd confide in; not a bit surprising. In fact, it's probably better that way—no one aunt or high school band director should have to deal with five troubled kids!

When you go to this next level, you'll want to make sure that the adults your children are talking to know the situation, know what they're dealing with, and know your take on the troubles and what you've told the children. One suggestion: Go over some of the ideas in this chapter with them.

Teens for Teens

There's one further resource for teen-agers, and it's a good one: other teen-agers. Teens are a clannish group; occasionally they can seem like another species. For some, at some times, grown-ups are alien, not to be trusted. A lot of teen-agers have told me that the only people they can talk with freely are their friends, *because only their friends understand what they're going through.* Some teens, at some times, won't talk to their own parents; they simply don't believe their parents can understand.

There could not be a more normal, more healthy response for teen-agers. So within the limits of family secrecy—of what *you're* comfortable having outside the house and in circulation—by all means, encourage your teen-agers to find comfort and confidants among their teen-age pals.

Artie Screws Up

Artie was eleven when his mom had the heart attack. It was massive; there was an all-out rescue effort. It took the best efforts of an outstanding cardiac care unit to save her life.

Because of some other physical problems, she couldn't go on a transplant standby right away. So for five weeks, her life had been sustained by a heart-mate, an electrical assist pump.

While she was on the heart-mate, her condition improved remarkably. She could walk around the hospital, work out on the treadmill, wear her own clothes. Of course, as long as her life depended on the machine, there was no question of discharging her from the hospital.

For her two children, the situation was a classic of medical crisis: Suddenly family members came rushing in from out of town; people were coming and going at all hours; the phone never stopped; good news alternated almost hourly with bad news.

Yet Artie's own situation seemed pretty good: He and his sister went to stay with an aunt and uncle whom they liked and who liked them; there were two other children in the house, and all of them got along fine. The family was extremely supportive, and Artie and his sister adapted quickly to the rules of the new household.

Artie's dad worked nights and visited Mom in the hospital every afternoon; nevertheless, he managed to spend some time with his children almost every day.

For Artie, it seemed, there was no problem.

One day, three or four weeks after the mother's heart attack, Artie's dad phoned me: "We've got to talk."

Artie, normally an A and B student, had just showed up with three Fs on his report card.

There had been no warning; Artie's quizzes were still coming home with As and Bs. What the father learned, in a series of agonized phone calls to teachers, was that Artie had simply stopped handing in his homework.

"Sometimes he's done it, sometimes he hasn't. But even when he's done it, he hasn't turned it in."

Artie, in fact, was doing just what a lot of kids in those circumstances do. He didn't realize it, but he was calling out for attention and help, and pretty effectively too.

On the surface, when Dad talked to him every day, Artie's reaction was always "I'm fine, I'm fine." Inside, he needed to let the world know "This whole thing is very difficult for me; I'm not handling it well." As we've seen, when your child is *not* "fine," school is one of the first places he'll show you.

Unscrewing Artie

Because the family was paying attention, some very important things happened in a hurry.

Artie afforded his family a few levers to adjust his conduct. Two things were very important to him: his baseball team and his karate lessons. In the midst of the medical crisis, the family had gone out of its way to make sure he could still have those two outlets. Now, Artie's aunt, working with his mom and dad, developed a plan. Artie agreed, and the school approved.

As I write this, Artie's plan is in effect. Every day he takes two home-made forms to school. On one he writes out every homework assignment in each class. Each teacher initials his assignment, signifying that Artie has got it right.

On the second form, the teachers indicate that Artie has turned in the previous day's assignment.

Only if both sheets are filled out and presented to Artie's aunt after school is he allowed to go to baseball practice and take his karate lesson. If either sheet were not filled out, he'd have to miss baseball or karate, and stay home and do the homework. I say "if" because so far Artie hasn't violated the terms of the agreement, not once. Since the new rules have been in effect, the dog has never eaten Artie's homework.

A couple of important things have happened.

First, Artie got the help, the *structure* he didn't know he needed. He would never acknowledge, or even understand, that he wasn't doing his homework because he was worried about his mom, because he was mad at the world for letting her get sick. Children like Artie don't have that kind of self-knowledge. For Artie there were just a lot of excuses: "I forgot—I left it in a book somewhere." And now there was a plan that, Artie agreed, would help him "remember" his homework. That's really all the understanding he needs.

Perhaps even more important to think about now was the involvement of Artie's *mother.*

Mom May Be Sick, But She's Still Mom

When Artie's dad first phoned me about those three Fs, I asked whether he'd talked to his wife about them. He said, "Good idea. She really knows Artie. I'll do that right now."

Remember, this was a woman who was functioning on half a heart. Nevertheless, *she was still Artie's mom. She still intended to be fully involved in his life,* heart machine or no heart machine. And that determination was absolutely vital *for both their needs.*

Mom needed to feel competent as a parent.

Artie needed to feel protected as a kid.

She and I have talked repeatedly about Artie's school problems, about the stress he's undergoing and how he handles it. Her husband is right; she is full of remarkable insights into her son.

It is a mistake for the well parent to try to shield the sick parent from involvement with the children.

Obviously, you can't and you won't try to push parenting on a mother or father who's just too wiped out to get involved. And you'll want to stay in close touch with the doctors as to how much is too much. Nevertheless:

- Many parents feel much better when they can come back, at least partially, into their parenting role.
- It is vital for the child that he continue to see his sick parent as a *parent.*

The more the child has to go without the sick parent's supervision, the less respect he will retain for the parent as parent—Mom is still Mom, and what she says goes. So:

Once you're out from under the acute crisis, once Mom or Dad is on treatment, recuperating, able to handle it, she or he needs to step back into a parenting role as quickly as possible. Because if the parent does not, the relationship with the child may *never* return to normal.

There's a remarkable little book I recommend, called *Moms Don't Get Sick.* (Aberdeen, South Dakota: Melius Publishing, 1990). It's co-written by Pat Brack, a mother who developed cancer, and her ten-year-old son Ben, and it recounts their experience of dealing together with her disease.

At one point, when Pat was still on chemotherapy and feeling absolutely terrible, Ben began to go wild, to break all the rules.

The defining moment came when his mother insisted he put on a pair of slippers, and Ben turned away and whispered, "Shut up!" Here is how Pat describes what happened next:

> I remember so clearly . . . my fury at Ben when he defied me and muttered, "Shut up." In that incoherent moment I realized how little discipline he'd been getting from me and how far I had let things slide. Energy born of rage and frustration took hold and I decided I would rather die instantly of overexertion than watch this once-lovable boy become an obnoxious little beast. A battle ensued. I found untapped energy enough to bounce him around the house . . .
>
> After this volcanic encounter, Ben put on his slippers and became very cheerful and loving. I think children need to feel that someone other than themselves is in control.

Even more significant is Ben's recollection of the "shut up" incident:

> Well, Mom heard and totally lost her temper. She picked me up and shook me and said she'd be dipped in chocolate before anybody told her to shut up. She backed me up and held me to the wall and told me that I would do exactly what she told me to do OR ELSE!! I went and got my slippers on fast. *I felt better than I had in a long time.* I think now that I back-talked on purpose *to see if Mom was really in there.* She sure was and that made me feel warm and safe. Later we hugged and made up. It was a wonderful day.

And that's what has to happen: The sick parent must show that even though she's sick, she's still Mom, and all her expectations for her children are intact and in place.

The Second Ripple of Help: School and Community Services

Because school is where so much of the trouble shows itself, it's a natural place to start looking for solutions. I've had some wonderful help from schools, and I've also had parents tell me they *didn't* get the help they expected. Let's talk about what your child's school needs from you now and what you should expect of the school.

Approaching the School for Help

By now you've probably already made the school aware of what's going on at home; if not, this is the time to do it. Start with a phone call, to find out exactly whom you can consult about helping your child through a family medical crisis. Usually it will be the guidance counselor; in some schools it will be the assistant principal. Sometimes a child's home-room teacher is assigned to be the child's liaison throughout the school day. In the lower grades, where the child has only one teacher, that teacher may be your primary contact. For simplicity's sake, I'll call whomever you're going to deal with "the counselor" from here on.

About the Counselor

In dealing with all kinds of counselors at all kinds of schools all over the Midwest, I've come to a few conclusions about them.

Guidance counselors in large, busy schools—even very good counselors—*must* focus on academic performance and behavior in school. That's what they're paid to do, and probably it's all they'll have time to do. So if school performance or acting-out with schoolmates is the problem, the counselor can be your first, and often your best, resource. But he or she is not employed to provide general counseling for children who are stressed *outside* of school life.

In big, urban schools, with underwhelming budgets and overwhelmed staffs, the counselor probably will intervene only in crisis cases—academic failure, truancy, and the like—and his or her focus will be narrow: to help with grades, period. Occasionally you'll run across the burned-out counselor who's just pulling time until retirement and is going to be very little help indeed. The more you know about your school and its guidance counselors, the better you'll be able to judge how much help you can expect.

In smaller, more intimate settings—good suburban schools, some private institutions—you can expect a great deal more. Counselors have more time and space for each student; frequently a counselor will take a stressed child under his or her wing, provide supportive one-on-one guidance well outside the narrow focus on school, stay in touch with the child, maybe even notice changes before you do. The counselor will become a friend.

All this is by way of suggesting that a school counselor can be a really good resource—perhaps all the help you need—or may offer very limited, restricted assistance. If that's the case, then you'll need to look a little further for help, either inside or outside the school.

Your First Meeting

First, make an appointment for a meeting. Even amid all the demands on your time right now, it's important for your child's welfare that this first conversation be face to face, not an impersonal chat over the phone.

Plan to bring your child along to that first meeting, where you'll discuss the problem that's bringing you here. It's important to include the child because:

- Just like you and me, children prefer to be talked *with* than to be talked *about.*
- You and the counselor need to hear your *child's* idea of the problem, which may be a little different from your own.
- You'll want the child's-eye view of the counselor.

At that meeting, you'll explain *your* perception of the problem—both to the counselor and to your child. Involve the child both in explaining the problem and in planning solutions. Say, for example: "It bothers Mom and me that you're fighting with your friends" or that "you're daydreaming during exams, and your grades show it," "you're forgetting words you already know how to spell," "you're not turning in your homework."

Whatever the problem, you and the counselor can begin to work out a solution, *with the child involved in the planning.* Artie's planning session, for instance, might sound like this.

"Artie, here's what we're thinking of doing. What if we worked up a printed form where you can write down homework assignments, and have your teachers initial that you've got them right? Then we can give you another form that they can initial each time you turn in your homework. And every time you give your aunt those forms, she'll let you go to baseball or to karate.

"Do you think that will work? Can you think of anything better, to get you over these homework troubles?"

Making Judgments

At any level of these ripples, the help you get will be only as good as the people who give it. In your meeting with the school counselor, or with any other resource, you'll begin, almost automatically, to make some judgments. If:

- You don't have a good feeling about this person
- The counselor doesn't really seem interested in your child
- The counselor seems defensive, telling you this problem is not the school's responsibility
- The counselor already seems to have negative feelings about your child
- You or your child have had conflicts in the past with this individual

then you may feel the need of going to someone else in the school. In a small elementary school, where your child has *just one teacher*, he or she is your obvious choice. But in the upper grades, your child probably has a whole roster of teachers, and it would be pretty hard to round up all of them.

The counselor's immediate superior is probably an *assistant principal or dean of students*—usually a person second in command to the principal.

In most schools the principal is probably too busy with budgets, school boards, and teachers' unions to cope effectively with one student's problems. But I find the assistant principal can often be of great assistance.

Don't hesitate to ask around among other parents as to who has proven helpful to them in the past and whom they'd just as soon bypass.

Making Sure It Happens

Once you've set up a plan with the school, whether it involves special supervision, tutoring, homework monitoring, whatever, you'll want to keep an eye out that it's really happening. At this point a lot of parents will trust the school personnel to implement the plan; that's probably naive.

Never assume that, just because you've set up a plan with a counselor or assistant principal, all your child's teachers have been properly notified and are on board. One counselor might send a detailed, written explanation of Artie's homework plan to every one of his teachers, asking for an acknowledgment by return interoffice mail. Another might simply mumble in a faculty meeting, "We're putting a homework check on Artie."

If you can find the time, try to confirm the plan by phone with each of your child's teachers. Have they seen it? Is it okay with them? Any additional ideas? There is nothing worse for your child than to agree to some kind of behavioral plan, only to find that one of the people who's supposed to be helping hasn't a clue as to what's going on. It's simply devastating to a child who's already on shaky ground.

Teacher Conflicts

What if your child has a teacher that he *really* doesn't like and doesn't get along with?

Under ordinary circumstances, you might keep hands off. After all, part of a child's education is learning to coexist with people—including teachers—whom he doesn't like very much. But now the circumstances are not ordinary; your child is dealing with the enormous stress of a parent's illness.

Academic problems suggest that the child is already having trouble maintaining his concentration, and it's a lot harder to concentrate on someone you don't want to listen to in the first place.

It's rare that a teacher conflict is so extreme that it becomes part of your child's problems, but it *does* happen.

If your child has a long-standing conflict with a teacher (which may not be either's fault) and his school performance is suffering, then you may want to talk about switching your child to a different class. Remember, because the parent's medical situation creates such extreme stress for the child, we try to reduce any other stresses we can.

Finally, if the school doesn't seem to be helping your child, if the plan isn't working and no one at the school seems able to come up with something better, then you're going to have to start looking beyond the school—to professional tutoring or counseling or even therapy.

Community Resources

A good place to start looking is right at the hospital. Whatever hospital you're involved with, it will certainly have a staff of social service workers and mental health specialists who can direct you toward the services you need—anything from community support groups to psychotherapists.

If you're closely involved with church or synagogue, ask your minister or rabbi whether he or she can recommend therapists or counselors.

There's another resource not many people think of, and it's right there by your phone: the local government section of your white pages or blue pages. Running down the list of community services in my phone book, I find such titles as:

Children, Office for
Family Guidance
Mental Health
Social Services

Simply call one that sounds like what you're looking for; if it isn't exactly the right office, it can direct you to the service you need.

Religious Resources

Your family's church or synagogue can open new avenues of help. There are youth and sports group leaders your children may like and trust, who can talk to them on the basis of considerable experience with kids in and out of trouble.

Priests, ministers, or rabbis often can be a great source of strength for a family in crisis. But unless they have special training in handling youngsters—and you're entitled to ask whether they do—they may *not* be the best resource for helping your troubled children.

Some may be awkward with children. Lacking special training, they may not know how to talk to a four-year-old, versus a seven-year-old, versus a teen-ager, about what's troubling them. Many clergy see their own roles as specifically dealing with the *spiritual* aspect of life's crises, not the behavioral or emotional aspects.

The clergymen and women of my experience are often very good at talking with children about the deep stuff—about the meaning of life, and why people have to die, and why life sometimes seems so unfair. But a child stressed by a parent's illness probably isn't worried about those things; she's upset about separation, she's dealing with anger, with a loss of parenting, with general fear of the unknown. Helping in those psychological situations requires special training. In *most* cases, I think, clergy are more a spiritual resource for the family than a ready source of help for troubled youngsters.

The Third Ripple of Help: Therapy

The ultimate layer of help is one you probably won't ever have to worry about. Most children will by this point have responded and be back on track toward normal—toward reasonable eating, comfortable sleep, good grades—toward reversing whatever behavior brought you to this chapter.

But if the answer to "What works?" is still "None of the above" and in the specific case of risky behavior, you may have to start thinking about psychotherapy—getting your child together with a psychologist or a psychiatrist. There's a lot of help available in finding one—your hospital counselor or social worker, your pediatrician, your school guidance counselor, the community service agencies you may already be in touch with.

In most communities you can find psychotherapists with special qualifications for working with children whose parents are very sick. One word of caution, however.

Nowadays many counselors and therapists are oriented to *family therapy*—their doctrine is to work with the entire family as a unit. You may decide that your family needs this approach. But in the situations we're talking about, it can be very rewarding for the child to see someone all alone, one on one. The problem you're dealing with is not the stress on the family but the stress on *this child.* And family counseling is one more demand on *your* time that you may not be able to handle right now.

Making Judgments

Once you go outside the circle of family and friends and begin looking for professional help, whether from a community guidance counselor or a psychotherapist, you're going to have to make certain judgments. The central one: *Will this person help?*

To a great extent, it's going to be a matter of gut instinct—whether you *feel* this person is right, or wrong, for you child. But a few guidelines may help.

The First Meeting

- Your child should be there. The child's judgment of this new person will be at least as important as yours. More important—particularly if we're dealing with a teen—he won't get the idea that something is going on behind his back. Help stamp out paranoia.
- The counselor or doctor should address your child by name. It's simple courtesy, and it demonstrates real interest.
- You should never have the feeling that the individual is talking

past your child, talking to you as if Danny weren't there. As an adult I find that offensive; to a child, it's a devastating put-down. The therapist should be either talking *to* Danny or looking over at him to make sure he feels part of the conversation. (That goes for you too, Mom or Dad—you never want to talk *about* your child as if the child weren't there. *He's there*—and all ears!)

- The therapist should use your child's name frequently; there should be a minimum of hims and hers—not "What about his eating disturbs you?" but "What about *Dan's* eating disturbs you?" Nobody wants to be a pronoun.
- The therapist should seek out your child's opinions. In my own practice, whenever the parent tells me of a problem—"I'm worried about Dan's schoolwork"—I'll usually turn right to Dan and say, "How about you—do *you* think you're having a problem at school?" The therapist should *want* to hear from your child—more, perhaps, than from you.
- You'll want to sense a rapport between the counselor and the child—a feeling that *both* are interested and will get along with each other. Above all, if after the get-acquainted session your son or daughter announces "I *hate* her," then it doesn't matter if the counselor is Mother Teresa or Dr. Spock—look further.

Results

Once you've taken on professional help, you judge its quality by what you see in your child. If he's going to a series of sessions, does he go happily; does he look forward to the time he'll spend with his new friend? Does he talk about the sessions? (especially with younger kids; teen-agers may not say one word about what's going on).

You must feel that this professional is keeping you well informed, both of progress and lack of progress. Probably you don't *want* to be involved on a session-by-session basis, but be sure you are comfortable with the level of involvement . . . with what you know and when you know it.

(One caution: Don't expect the therapist to share your child's confidences with you. Doctor-patient confidentiality is just as important for your children as for you. Your child must know that whatever she shares of herself with the doctor is safe with the doctor—that it *won't* get back to you, unless the *child* says that's okay. Without that absolute trust, that confessional seal, the therapy isn't going to work).

After that, it's a matter of results, over time. Is the eating or sleeping or performance problem that brought you into this beginning to go away? Probably the answer will be yes—if not, then talk to the therapist about why things aren't working out. And get answers that satisfy *you.*

HELP!: A SUMMARY

You've identified a problem or a pattern of negative behavior in your child. We'll start at the center: you and your child together, then look at the widening circles of help available:

At the Center: You and Your Child:

- How to "fish" for answers to your questions (page 80)
  - Questions *not* to ask
  - The right kind of questions
  - Questions about specific problems that worry you
- What to do when your kids lose some of your parenting (page 83)
  - Help them bring out their emotions
  - Encourage physical activity
  - Encourage disciplined sports
- Teaching your children how to relax mind and body (page 85)
- Laughter as medicine (page 87)
  - When to laugh, when to be serious: let the child be your guide
- What to do when you *can't* make it better for them (page 88)
- When to get tough (page 89)

The First Circle of Outside Help: Family and Friends

- When your kids can't talk to you: gender problems (page 90)
- When you're too stressed to help your children (page 90)
- Whom can they turn to? Ask them! (page 90)
- A major resource: teens for teens (page 91)
- This is important: Keep the sick parent involved (page 94)

The Second Circle of Outside Help: School and Community

- How to approach the school for help (page 96)
- Some guidance about guidance counselors (page 96)
  - First meeting: What to do, what to look for (page 97)

Ways you can judge the counselor (page 98)
What if you're not satisfied? (page 98)

- Include your child in any school planning (page 98)
- Trust but verify: Make sure the plan happens (page 99)
- What if your child has a teacher conflict? (page 99)
- Community resources: But where do you find them? (page 100)
- Religious resources: some thoughts (page 101)

The Final Circle of Outside Help: Therapy

If it's needed, it will usually be short-term. We're talking about a problem arising because of the parent's medical crisis, not something more deep-rooted:

- Some ideas on how to find the therapy your child may need (page 101)
- Judging the therapist, and the therapy: some guidelines (page 102)
- Some thoughts about results (page 103)
- About confidentiality between therapist and child (page 103)

FIVE

Preparing Children for Hospital Visits

Two Kinds of Visits

Take a moment to look at the picture on the following page; I love it!

The artist was a nine-year-old girl who went to see her dad in the intensive care unit, then drew what she'd seen. The drawing is just about textbook-accurate; every piece of medical equipment hooked up to her father is correctly drawn and in the right place. We even get to see half of the patient next door—the artist knew she wasn't supposed to look at him, but she couldn't resist a peek.

What this picture tells me is that this little girl isn't scared, not one bit. She's taking in everything she sees and handling it with a good reporter's eye for accuracy. She shows us that she understands what's happening to her father and that all that scary stuff is really good stuff because it's there to help him. Because she understands, she's handling her feelings. Instead of being frightened, she's *interested.*

I'm showing it to you for the same reason I show it to parents who consult me—to demonstrate that *you don't have to protect your*

children from medical experiences. You just have to prepare them. In this chapter we'll talk about two different kinds of hospital visits children make.

First, there are visits to parents in intensive care units, where the medical situation is never less than serious and ranges on up to life-threatening. Second, there are visits to parents in non–life-threatening situations—a trauma unit after a car accident; the dialysis unit for kidney work.

It's all the same hospital but, for young visitors, the two situations must be handled entirely differently.

Preparing for Critical-care and Intensive-care Visits

The sight of a seriously ill parent in a hospital critical care unit is frightening, and we must start off understanding that. All the masks are gone, even those minimal little cosmetic aids with which we face our loved ones daily—a shave, combed hair, shaped eyebrows, dentures. What remains is a pallid husk, hooked up to a terrifying array of catheters, drips, and monitors. How can we even think of inflicting such a sight on a child?

The answer is, once again, your child is *entitled.* The more menacing the situation, the more important for your child's future well-being that he have this opportunity—perhaps this final opportunity—to visit, if he wants to. That's still Dad or Mom on the other end of all that hardware, and most children are going to want to go. (Some won't, and that's okay. It's a decision best left to the child.) And I can assure you, most children who want to visit can handle the visit just fine—we simply have to prepare for it.

Reacting Where It's Safe

The first consideration: If the child is going to react emotionally, you want him or her to react someplace safe—*not* in the hospital's intensive care unit. I've been called, more times than I like to remember, to deal with a little boy or girl who's run screaming from the first, unanticipated sight of Dad or Mom.

And yet children, especially school-age children, are very curious about medical apparatus and absolutely fascinated with bodies—their own and other people's.

So the answer is to prepare the child for exactly what he's going to see, to let him go through all the yecchs and "Oh, gross"es safe at home—and to brace yourself for some pretty unsentimental reactions.

("What did they do with Dad's old liver? Is it in a jar somewhere? *Can we see?*" School-age kids are *fascinated* with mutilation!)

Dress Rehearsal

Sit down with your children in advance. Explain exactly what Mom or Dad looks like today; you might even sketch that there's an I.V. drip here because Mom or Dad can't eat yet, a huge bandage covering where the doctors went in to take out the tumor, a breathing tube into the mouth. Let your children know just what they're going to see *before* they walk in on it.

If the parent is really sick, taking a Polaroid photograph to show the children can be a terrific help—just be sure that the hospital staff says it's okay and won't compromise the parent's medical situation. Go over the picture with the children, explaining exactly what's going on and what each piece of equipment is for.

You can help prepare young children with a doll: "The doctors had to cut Daddy's hair, so they could get to the tumor in his head. Shall we cut Raggedy Andy's hair, and see what he looks like?" Tape lengths of tubing or fishing line to a doll to show where catheters are going and what they're for.

Keep in mind: The older the child, the more preparation he or she may need before going to see a parent whose appearance is dramatically altered. "Mom really looks different now, because of the surgery. Just remember that she's still Mom, and she still loves you. Everything else is just the surface."

Preparing for the Emotions

It's important to prepare children, not just for what they'll see, but for what they'll *feel* when they visit a parent in intensive care—especially a parent whom they haven't seen for a while. What they'll see may make them feel frightened, may make them feel like crying. And all those feelings are *okay*.

When we get very ill, we don't look much like those very ill people in the movies and the daytime soap operas—fetchingly pale, with just a little hint of pain at the corner of a clear blue eye. We look *scary*.

The patient in renal failure is frighteningly swollen. The body that is rejecting a bone marrow graft may break out in unsightly rashes. And even though the child may be forewarned, the reality can overcome his preparation.

The problem is more severe with an unresponsive or unconscious parent. The parent who is in command, who can say, "Well, hi," as you walk into the room, can engage the child's interests and demonstrate that Mom or Dad is still "in there," despite appearances.

But a parent whose appearance is seriously altered, and particularly one who can't repond, may trigger an overwhelming wave of fear or grief even in a child who's been well prepared. So part of that preparation should be:

"Now, when you see Mom, it may be hard for you to handle. You may just want to cry, you may want to leave the room. However you feel, *that's okay, sweetie*. Don't be afraid, don't be ashamed. If you want to cry, I'm here to hold you. If you want to leave the room for a while, that's what we'll do. Mom will understand; I'll understand."

(And you want to be sure that the sick parent *does* understand. Warning *her* how her child may react—explaining the content of this section—is a crucial part of preparing for the child's visit.)

If, after this kind of preparation, your child decides that, well, maybe I don't want to do this right now, that's fine. But if, as is more likely, she still wants to visit Mom, then you've done it right—you've given her the preparation she'll need, not only for what she's going to see, but also for what she's going to feel.

The Visit Itself

In planning the visit itself—and a child's visit to a critical care unit *needs* to be planned—keep three points in mind:

1. **It should be the *child's* visit, planned around him or her. If you, Mom, want to get and give the comfort of just holding your husband's hand silently for half an hour, do that another** time. Don't plan on leaving the room to talk with a doctor or a nurse or a social worker. Your child's visit is for your child. You're there for support.

2. Plan the specifics of the visit—and *make sure in advance that what you want for the children is okay with the medical staff.* That may mean conferring with the doctor; more often you'll talk to the head nurse, who is in continuous contact with the patient and sympathetic to family needs. And most children like to meet the doctor and nurses who are caring for their mom or dad.

Then explain to your children exactly what's going to happen and what they may do:

"It's okay to touch Daddy; you can go over and squeeze his hand. He'll like that.

"Now, he has a tube in his mouth, so he can't talk to you. But I know he'll want to listen; he'd love to hear about you guys winning the ball game yesterday.

"And if you want me to, I'll pick you up and you can give Daddy a kiss too, even though he may not be able to kiss you back. Okay?"

Don't go into the unit with any specific expectations. It's all right for the children to kiss the sick parent, but it's also all right for them *not* to. You make the suggestions; let them decide.

3. Plan a brief visit—and, odd as it may seem, the *older* the child, the *shorter* the visit. Here's why:

Very young children, who don't fully understand what's going on, will be fine playing with their toys for a while around the foot of Dad's bed. But once the older child has had his visit with Daddy, his imagination will begin to wander—that array of tubes and beeping monitors is going to start overwhelming him, terrifying him with the menace of the unknown.

So: Plan to fill the time and then leave; don't give your kids empty minutes to start imagining bad things.

A Visit to Mom

Every rule, of course, creates its own exceptions. This is the story of a visit that broke the keep-it-short rule, a visit that went on and on—and why that was a good thing.

She was in severe respiratory difficulty. She'd been in our intensive care unit for three weeks, unable to breathe on her own. A tracheal tube kept her alive, but she'd contracted pneumonia, then a series of other infections. She was slipping in and out of consciousness; it wasn't clear at this point whether she would recover, remain at some midpoint neither sick nor well, or finally succumb as one infection followed another.

She had three sons: Curtis was three, Johnny was seven, and Billy was nine. As is so often the case, each had his own needs and his own issues to resolve.

The big problem was Johnny.

Little Curtis seemed really comfortable at the hospital, as many young children are. He wasn't afraid of the daunting apparatus surrounding his mom, nor of his mom's medical condition. For one thing, she'd been sick for most of his short life; this wasn't a big change. For another, he'd been staying with his mom's parents, and Grandma had been bringing him in regularly to visit.

But the older boys had been staying with Dad, and this was their first visit to Mom in the ICU. Their father really hadn't grasped how vital it was, not only for the boys to see her but, perhaps even more important, for Mom to see her boys.

Dad and the two older boys arrived late; we had only a short time to tell them what to expect. And Dad had someplace he had to be afterward; the visit was really getting squeezed.

What immediately became obvious was that seven-year-old Johnny was terrified of the ICU. He arrived scared; people in the family had told him, "Mommy's going to die." He hung back, standing far away from the bed, wanting nothing to do with this frightening-looking creature with all the tubing—this creature who hardly resembled his mom at all.

After three weeks, Mom desperately needed contact—close, physical contact—with both her older boys. But Johnny hid around a corner in the entrance hall, occasionally peeking out at his mom for an instant, then pulling back again.

Billy, the nine-year-old, did better. He was, of course, more mature and more verbal than Johnny. Billy walked in and said "Hi" to his mom. Initially he was a bit scared; that's typical. But soon he relaxed, reached out, touched Mom, and started talking to her.

(You'll know when a child begins to relax and get more comfortable. You'll see him start to look around, take things in. Finally he'll begin to ask questions. That's when the crunch is over).

After a few minutes, with Johnny still hiding around the corner, his dad decided enough was enough and reached out to pull him into the room. I said, "No, don't do that." This was a time for patience. The important thing was, Johnny was *not* saying "I want to go now." When a child insists on leaving, it's best to leave and try again another time. But when the child is willing to stick around, that's important, and you can work with it if you let him take it at his own speed. Johnny was obviously being pulled between his mom and his fears, and he needed time to decide which way he would go.

At this point something very good happened: Billy went over to talk to his younger brother. "Mom and I are having fun together!" He even played a little childhood psychology on Johnny: "I'm going to get something you're not. Mom's giving me part of her lunch!"

Now Dad recognized that what was happening with Johnny was a lot more important than any appointment; everybody stayed.

After a while, I got Johnny talking about what he was seeing around the corner, about what was scary to him. And finally Johnny said, "Well, I'll come in, but *just once, just for a minute!*" I said that would be just fine.

The more we empowered him, the more we let him make his own decisions, the more things he said he would try. First he started around the corner and ducked back again. But then he came out, tiptoed into the room, and whispered, "I love you, Mommy." He backed up then, but not quite to the corner. And now he couldn't help noticing: His older brother was holding Mom's hand; the nurse at the bedside was chatting him up. Billy was making himself at home, getting a lot of neat attention. Johnny was starting to feel a little left out.

Johnny had made a picture for Mom. Now suddenly he walked forward, right up to her bedside, and put the picture down on the blanket, then backed away a step. *And that was as close as Johnny came, on this visit.* Mom obviously wanted and needed to reach out and hold him, but that would have scared him away again. I told her, "By the next visit, Johnny will be a lot more comfortable."

And he was. The next time he came he let his mother take his hand. He was still passive, still staring fixedly, unwilling to acknowledge the environment of the ICU. But on the third visit Johnny strolled into the room, walked straight over to his mother, took her hand, and began to look around.

From what I could find out, he suffered no ill effects; there were no bad dreams, no eating problems, none of the warning signs of trouble. Time and patience had taken care of Johnny, and they took care of his mom too—eventually she was transferred to a rehabilitation hospital to begin the long, difficult road to recovery. Her life was no longer in danger.

After the Visit

Despite your best efforts at preparation, the sight of a parent in intensive care can be a severe shock to any child. A father whose face seems swollen to twice its size after brain surgery, a mother gray and wan and shrunken, can simply overwhelm the child's preparation and defenses.

If you know the parent in intensive care looks very different from when the children last saw him, it's a good idea to bring along a favorite picture, from the good times. Then, if you see the child badly upset after the visit, sit down with her there in the hospital lounge and tell her the truth about the future: "You know, after a while, Daddy is going to be back just the way he was. Remember how he looked before all this? I have a picture here; let's look at it and remember things. . . ."

What If Your Child Doesn't Want to Go to the Hospital?

If your child does decide, no, I'm not going to see Dad in the hospital, then it's important for you to offer alternatives. Because pretty certainly, if the child is past toddlerhood, he's thinking, somewhere inside, "I *should* go." What's important now is to head off any guilt—which is likely to make an even worse mess later on.

Frequently I'll suggest that the child draw a special picture that I can take to the parent. I promise to tape it to the wall where Dad can see it. Or I'll ask, "Would you like to take a walk with me outside and pick a flower I can take to Dad?"

Another possibility for an older child, if the sick parent is mentally alert, is to write a letter or a special poem.

Here is a poem that was written by a nine-year-old named Kevin, for his mother, who was coming home from the hospital. Her condition was terminal.

Your sons and your spouse
Love and care for you
Every day as you go through the Valley of Shadows;

There's a ruler over all:
He's the creator of the world;
He made you and me walk together.

Together we'll be for eternity;
Even though we may split apart,
We'll always be together through the heart.

Come home now, and stay in God's care.

Preparing for Non–Critical-Care Visits

Being treated in a hospital's non–critical-care areas is serious enough, painful perhaps, unpleasant certainly—but *your life is not threatened.* It's almost a different hospital . . . a more relaxed, lower-tech, far less threatening hospital. And for children visiting parents in these non–critical-care units, it's an entirely different situation from the intensive-care areas.

- Visits can be longer—a lot longer. They can, in fact, become family occasions . . . a bit of home away from home for everyone.
- Almost certainly, the patient will be able to talk with the children, to keep up conversations, perhaps even play games. Of course, if there's been a serious (if temporary) change in appearance, you might want to do an abbreviated version of the advance preparation we talked about in "Dress Rehearsal." But unless there's an initial shock of appearance, you can probably leave it to the patient to explain any medical equipment that may be hooked up.
- You can suggest that your children bring along homework to do, or a backgammon set or a deck of cards. The sick parent may be delighted to have her kids there, but she certainly doesn't want to spend the whole time entertaining them. And for a kid, talking to somebody sick—even somebody sick whom you love—can get pretty boring. So make sure the visiting children have plenty to occupy their time—TV can help.

  I've had families set up picnics right beside Mom's bed. (Let the kids plan the menu.) I've known some to bring in pizzas!
- Holidays and birthdays can be celebrated right at bedside; again, the kids can plan the miniparty.

Kids to the Rescue

Just because the situation isn't life-threatening doesn't mean that children's visits aren't important. They can be absolutely crucial, both for the children and for a sick mom or dad:

He was young, he was good-looking, he was successful, he had a pretty wife and two super kids—and now he might be about to lose his leg.

He'd been in a car crash, been taken first to a local hospital for treatment of a badly mangled leg. When it failed to respond, he was medevaced to our trauma unit.

He hadn't seen his eight-year-old daughter and six-year-old son in two weeks. *And he didn't seem to want to.*

The children, staying with an aunt back home, were growing concerned, were starting to feel cut off. Yet their mother told a nurse she was worried about having them come visit. Her husband was depressed, in great fear of losing his leg. Above all, he didn't want his children to see him like this.

I went to talk with him and he told me, "I'm trying to keep a good attitude, I really am. But *what's my life going to be like if I lose my leg?* My kids will be embarrassed by me. How can I teach my boy to play football? How can I do any of the things that I assumed were part of my life?"

He saw the loss of the leg as so *huge.* He truly feared that his children would reject him, be grossed-out by a one-legged father. I suspect he had some of the same fears about his beautiful young wife, even though she'd been demonstrating right along that there wouldn't be a problem. I believed he was missing a point: His wife and children didn't love his leg; they loved *him.*

I talked with his kids on the phone. They seemed to have a good grasp of what was happening. They didn't appear to be afraid, although they showed a lot of anger at the driver of the other car.

The mother told me she was terribly worried. She thought it would be good for her husband to have the children come, but he was *so* depressed. What if he snaps at them? What if he ignores them? What if he makes them feel rejected?

It was a toss-up. The children were eager to see their dad, but they seemed to be okay; they were showing no warning signs of trouble to come. Nevertheless, my suggestion was that they come and come now—not so much for them, but for him. He needed to see his children and to see whether they would reject him or not. So his wife and I pushed the visit and finally, reluctantly, he agreed.

She and I briefed the children carefully. We explained what they would see—the leg was open, badly infected. We warned them about the odor; it wasn't overwhelming, but it was definitely there.

But what we really emphasized was how Dad was feeling emotionally. He was scared of the operation that might take away his leg. We made sure they understood that that was a real possibility, even though the doctors were doing everything they could to avoid amputation.

"Your dad's pretty discouraged now. He's been through a lot of pain, had to switch hospitals, been far away from you guys. He's feeling down, and Mom thinks you can help cheer him up."

That was the idea that caught their imagination: *You can help your dad.* They arrived at the hospital almost with a sense of mission.

When they came into the room, they were fine; they weren't afraid of anything they saw. And you could watch them take on this adult role. These were good kids of good parents; Mom and Dad had given them the strength to handle this situation long before it arose. I believe what happened next made a great difference in their dad's orientation and in his recovery.

They started right off, telling him about what was going on in their lives and what they wanted him to get back to. He responded slowly, rather hesitantly to this cheerful chatter.

Finally the children said very clearly: "We really miss you. We want you home. No matter what happens, Daddy, if they can fix your leg or if they have to take it away, we still want you home. We'll do everything we used to do. It'll be a little different, but it'll be okay."

The young father had been terribly depressed, yet since the accident he had never cried. Now, listening to his children, he cried—a warm, relieving kind of crying. He reached out both arms and cradled them. Behind them, his wife was crying too. Amid the tears, you watched this family come together again.

Finally he could talk, could express his feelings. "I've been really scared. And I really missed you guys."

When I visited again, later in the day, I found him playing checkers with his daughter. A very ordinary bedside scene.

The young man did not lose his leg; the surgeons were able to restore circulation and he is now in long-term rehabilitation. Chances are he'll wind up with a pretty good leg.

When It's Better Not to Go

There are situations when it's just as well for the child *not* to visit the hospital.

If the parent's appearance is really pretty bad—especially if the parent can't respond—and *if the child is handling the situation fairly well* then you may decide to discourage a visit, or at least postpone it. Seeing a parent who looks dreadful, who may be unconscious or comatose—it will be very hard to make such a visit valuable for a child. Unless the situation is about to change dramatically—unless this may be the *last* visit—it's probably just as well for the child not to see the ill parent right now.

But if the child is *not* handling the situation well, if she's becoming suspicious, wondering what you might be keeping from her, *wondering whether Dad is even still alive*—then, with a lot of preparation, you should take her to see for herself.

Usually, as you've seen, I encourage children to go to the hospital—especially if the parent is in a life-threatening situation. Be sure to check with the hospital in advance, but most will bend visitation rules regarding children when there might be no further chances to see a gravely ill parent . . . or when a child needs to see for herself that the parent really is still alive.

The decision isn't always simple, however, and the first instinct isn't always the best. Let me leave you with a story of a family that really needed to see a beloved, and very sick, father—and why, in the end, they agreed not to.

I've mentioned this family before: a girl fifteen, a boy eleven, a girl nine, whose father suffered a massive heart attack and who was put on a heart-mate—an artificial pump—the only way to keep him alive until a donor heart became available.

The mother had been honest with the children, up to a point. She told them at once that their father had suffered a heart attack, that he was in the cardiac-care unit, and that he was being sustained by a machine. But the children were so upset that she stopped there. She decided that the wrenching part about the need for a heart transplant could keep for another couple of days. She decided she'd tell them the rest on Monday, before school.

On Sunday the mother and children went to church. And the priest asked the congregation to pray for a fellow parishioner who was gravely ill *and awaiting a heart transplant.*

It was nothing but a series of failures of communication; the priest had no idea that the children didn't know about the transplant part. But the children were furious at their mother: "You didn't tell us about a heart transplant!"

When she came to see me Tuesday, the mother said glumly, "My kids think I'm lying to them now."

By the time I talked with the children, they'd pretty well accepted that their mother hadn't deceived them, that she really did intend to tell them about the transplant, but events got ahead of her. But there it was: the beginning of distrust.

At this point, all three wanted to visit their dad. In the back of their minds, I think, they wanted to make sure that he really was still alive. And when it will help the children, nurses are usually willing to bend the rules. But:

In this case the father's condition was extremely precarious. His doctors didn't want him stimulated in any way. They wanted not even the slightest change in blood pressure or in breathing rate. They wanted him no more alert than the twilight sleep state they were holding him in with medication. Too, with his chest open for the heart-mate connection, there was a serious danger of infection—a danger heightened by every person who might come near him.

So in this case, the medical risk to the father had to outweigh the psychological risk of the children *not* seeing him. For one thing, the gravest risk of all to the children would be if they *did* see him and something went wrong after their visit.

I told them all that—told them that even the germs that couldn't make *them* sick might make *him* sick. I told them that the spiritual part within his sleeping body might sense that they were there, might try to wake up a little to respond to them, look at them, smile at them. Just the pleasure of hearing their voices might make him try to wake up.

And I explained that the doctors didn't want him waking up even the slightest bit; they wanted him to stay fast asleep under medication, so he wouldn't strain the little bit of heart muscle he had left.

All three understood and agreed that it would be better *not* to see him. Most important, at the end of the explanation, all three *knew* their father was still alive.

And so we talked some more, and finally the nine-year-old asked the question that *had* to be answered: "Could he die?" Mom's answer was "We just have to pray." But, as you understand by now, that was not an answer; the question remained open. And so when, at the end of our session, I said, "Do you have any other questions?" the younger daughter asked again, "Could he die from this?"

That is a question I always try to have children answer from within themselves. So I asked: "What do *you* think?"

"Yes," she said after a moment. "I think he could die from this." The other two both nodded.

Now we all knew.

*P*REPARING FOR HOSPITAL VISITS: A SUMMARY

A general rule: If the child wants to visit a sick parent, and the hospital staff says okay, it's usually good for *both* the child and the parent.

Here's a quick list of considerations to help you decide whether the child should visit:

- Does the child want to go?
- Does the sick parent want a visit?
- Can the sick parent tolerate a visit, medically? (The doctor or nurse must decide.)
- Will the hospital permit a visit by a minor child? Check the regulations, then talk to the staff about special arrangements.

Two Kinds of Visit: They're Very Different (page 108)

- Critical-care units
- Non–critical-care units

Preparing Children to Visit Critical-Care Units (page 110)

- Why should they visit? (page 110)
- Prepare them at home for what they'll see (page 111)
    - How to use drawings and photographs (page 111)
    - What to tell them (page 111)
    - Preparing for their emotions (page 111)
    - The visit itself: remember three key points (page 112)
        - It's the *child's* visit
        - You should plan what will happen
        - Keep the visit *brief*
- After the visit: dealing with a shock (page 116)
- If the child decides *not* to visit (page 116)
    - Handling the guilt
    - Sending a token: flowers, pictures, poems

Preparing Children to Visit Non–Critical-Care Areas **(page 117)**

- A different set of rules
- Things to do at bedside

Two Memories

Kids to the rescue (page 118)
When it was better not to go (page 120)

Remember: to make the visit a good one:

- Prepare your child thoroughly for what she'll experience
- Give her specific jobs or activities to do during the visit (decorating a wall, telling the sick parent something that happened)
- Explain the kind of emotions—fear, sorrow—people may have when they visit in the hospital

Six

Coming Home

"Can You Stop by My Office for a Few Minutes?"

Whenever one of our patients is about to be sent home after treatment, I like to spend an hour or so with the well parent to talk about what's likely to happen now and especially how the children may be affected. If you could actually come to my office, we'd probably chat along these lines:

> I just heard the good news—your wife has finished her treatment and will be coming home in a day or two.
>
> Your kids have been real good about all this—they've visited Mom in the hospital, and all of them have been handling their lives very well—they're in school and doing fine. But now things are going to change for them again, and it's probably not going to be the change they expect.
>
> Most kids, and especially the little ones, expect that as soon as Mom comes home, she'll be just fine, ready to start up all the Mom things right away. You know the reality.
>
> She's feeling the effects of her treatment; she's lost her hair, she's losing weight, her energy level right now is zilch and it's not going to improve very much for a while.

So even before she comes home, it's really important that your children understand she's not going to be 100 percent the mom they remember. I'd suggest that, *before you bring her home,* you sit down with the children and explain how she's going to feel. Have her explain too, next time they come to visit. In fact, this would be a very good time to start having *family meetings.*

Regular Family Meetings

You might make a plan for sitting down, all together as a family, perhaps once a week, perhaps even more often. Set a regular time and place. Get everyone together—including your wife if she feels up to it—and update the children on any changes that are going on.

You'll want to tailor the length of the meetings, and how much information you try to get across, to the kids themselves. A two-hour family meeting might be okay for teen-agers; it's far too long for young children. You know about how much your kids can absorb at any one time.

The First Meeting

Talk about what it will be like when Mom comes home:

- How she'll feel.
- Will she sleep in her regular room or some special place?
- Will any special equipment come home with her? When is it coming? What does it look like? What will it do for her?
- Any questions?

You'll find your children will handle things a lot better if you give them time to prepare for what's going to happen.

Especially, let your children know what to expect in terms of how Mom will feel and what her abilities and limitations will be in the first few days and weeks. Prepare them for the fact that Mom will be going through a big adjustment. Make it concrete for them. Say, for example:

"Remember how it felt when you had the flu? Everything's normal, then suddenly you're real sick. You go to bed, and for three or four days you feel totally rotten, then you get a little better. So you try to get back into normal life, but everything feels weird. You feel out of body, out of sync, not even sure where everything is in your own house?

"Well, Mom's been in the hospital for *three weeks,* going through some pretty rough treatment, so being back home is going to be really strange to her for a while. She's going to be disoriented, and she may seem a little weird.

"And . . . Mom's looking at her life a lot differently now; she's asking herself a lot of questions about values, about what things mean. *She's not going to be the same. . . .*"

Your children need information about all those things, so they're prepared, so they understand why *Mom is still a little different,* and why it will take a while for things to get back to as normal as they will get. And how normal will that be?

What to Expect Now

If the doctors tell you to expect complete recovery, reassure your children that things *will* get back to normal and give them the time frame—Mom will be all better, but it's going to take a while—by Christmas—by next summer—maybe even a year.

If things will always be different, then the children need to begin to understand what the differences will be. And coming to that understanding is a *process.* You don't achieve it in one meeting. You get there slowly, over time. (We'll talk about that in the next chapter, on chronic illness.)

If recovery will be slow, and especially if the disease is likely to recur, the children *must* be forewarned. Because if they expect the disease never to come back, and it does, this will be a huge disappointment, with serious consequences for them. It may be worse than the first time, because now they know exactly what to expect. They may even blame Mom for getting sick again. So right now is the time to give them all the bad news, along with the good.

Getting Ready for the Homecoming

The kids can help you get ready for Mom's homecoming and help prepare themselves at the same time. They already know she's lost her hair because of the chemotherapy, so take them shopping on Saturday. Let them pick out half a dozen gorgeous headscarves. For a while, at least, she's not going to be able to pull knit tops over her head, or button anything in back, so have the kids select some pretty blouses that button in front. (For ideas on how the children can help out once Mom is home, go back to Chapter 2.)

No Big Deal, Please

For the sake of everybody—your wife, your kids, yourself—I'd suggest you keep the homecoming very low key. There's a tendency to have a big party: Resist it. Lots of family and friends are going to want to celebrate her return, especially with a good prognosis. But:

Your children really need private time with their parents in your own family environment.

It's fine for people to drop by, fine for friends to help you out, but *don't do it as a huge celebration.* Give yourselves a little time. Understand that your children need privacy too. If people start trooping incessantly through your home to see your wife, the children are going to feel intruded upon.

In any case, they may need some understanding—permission to go to friends' houses, permission to go to their rooms and keep the doors closed for a while. *Every child in every family needs a private space where he or she can be alone and know the space won't be violated.*

This is especially true for your older kids—the teens. They are really going to need their privacy now. No kid wants home to be Grand Central Station, and a lot of youngsters in this situation tell me that's exactly how they feel—a house full of people hanging around trying to be helpful.

Remember that when you need it, there's nothing like the good old answering machine as a crowd-control device: "Hi. This is an update: Wendy is doing fine. The doctors say she'll be up in a few days. We're just going to be a nuclear family tonight; so thanks for the call and please leave a message, because Wendy and I both want to get back to you."

Letting Teachers and Schools Know

One more thing you'll need to do is go to your children's schools and tell their teachers Mom is coming home or is already home. (If your wife feels well enough, perhaps she'll want to make the contacts by phone. But one of you should do it, and soon).

The teachers should understand that things will probably be a little different—Mom's home, but she's going to be on the kids' minds. Basically, give the teachers the same kind of information you did when your wife was first diagnosed. Most important, explain that while any help or comfort—from teachers or friends—will be appreciated, *there must be no compromise on what is expected of your children by the school.*

You will allow no easing up on academic demands, no "compassionate grading," above all, *no permission to fail.* All your children's teachers must understand: You and your wife will accept no compromise on achievement, and if there's a problem, you want to be notified immediately.

Let the teachers know that you'll keep them up to date and then do so from time to time. Teachers are going to be some of your best resources, and most helpful allies, through these weeks or months or years of stress on your children.

Continuing the Family Meetings

Some families have meetings only around new medical crises. That's okay, but I strongly recommend *regular* meetings that don't carry an aura of emergency. Periodic, scheduled meetings assure your kids that they're in the loop, being briefed regularly and openly. When the patient is up to it, meetings let the children hear from both parents together, so they aren't tempted to manipulate one of you against the other.

But on a more basic level, family meetings make *all* your children, even the little ones, feel more mature and responsible. They see that you consider their input important. They know that grown-ups, Dad and Mom, have regularly gone off to important meetings. Now there's a family meeting: *It must be important.*

Spell Out What's Expected of Everyone

A lot has probably changed while Mom was away, so in the first couple of meetings, you need to remind the kids of what you and your wife expect: who does what chores; bedtimes; behavior; house rules. Address the situation very honestly: We know Grandma didn't make you clean your rooms, but Mom's home now, and we want to get back to the way things were.

You and your wife have to confer about the rules, think about which ones you might want to modify, make a plan. Remember: *Your children will do best if they have the security of getting back to a normal routine as much as possible, as soon as possible.*

Schedule Private Time

Meetings or no, each child is going to need some private time with you and some private time with Mom. It's really important that you and your wife build that into your days. You're going to be pulled in a million directions now, *but the kids still need some time with each of you.*

Watch for ways you can incorporate that private time into the routine. If your teen-age son has the job of washing the car each Saturday, you can go out there with him, catch up with what's going on at school and with his girlfriend (unless he just *hates* washing the car; then it's a good time for you *not* to be around!). Remember, too, that you and your partner need and deserve time with each other—*without* the kids.

Family meetings are more for information and reassurance; your kids won't share their feelings then. It's going to be in private, one on one, that they'll share. You know what times they're most communicative—one may tend to confide at night, just before going to sleep; another gets very thoughtful in the morning, over cereal. So try to zero in on those times and find a moment to say "I just wanted to see how you're doing. Got any questions about Mom? How are things going? Are you getting back to normal at school? Got any plans for the weekend? How was the Brownies meeting?"

Just chat with them about their feelings and activities—touch base with them. *They'll really need that from you.* They're going to need some private time with Mom too; you and she together have to balance that need against not wearing her out.

Each child needs to find a time alone with her, when they're not competing for her attention. Especially your quieter kids—they're likely to be less assertive, to stand back and wait for someone to invite them.

When you see your children doing that, you need to open that door, to say "I have to work in the garage for a bit; can you sit with Mom? I think she'd enjoy the company." You need to help it happen. And of course, you need to be sure Mom is up to it. The two of you should do a little plotting together.

Watching for Signs of Trouble—Again

Both of you must *watch for behavior changes in your children*—those signs of trouble we talked about at the beginning of all this. (See Chapter 3, "Early Warnings.")

Trust your gut: If you think one of the children looks worried or distracted; if she's angry at everything when there's nothing to be angry at—you may not be able to figure out what's wrong, but *chances are something is wrong.* Try to find a way to get at it. *But don't try during the time your child is really upset.* Wait until a quiet time, when the child is open to you.

Dads' Laps and Moms' Laps

Remember, we're talking about behavior that continues over time. There will be moments when your children appear sad; children's emotions go on incredible roller-coaster rides.

Being sad for a short period of time is perfectly okay. At some point, you're going to come into a room and see your child wipe away tears real quick, and say everything's fine. And you'll know he was just crying. Go put an arm around him, give him a hug or a squeeze or a pat on the backside, whatever is comfortable for both of you, and say, "If you want to talk about it, I'm here, but if you just want a hug, I'm here for that too."

The kids don't really have to understand; they'll just have these down moments. They don't even need to talk—just to know you're there for them, and you'll do whatever is needed to try to make them feel secure.

I like to remember a lovely line in a lovely book called *A Taste of Blackberries* (by Doris B. Smith; New York: HarperCollins Children's Books, 1988), when a little boy says:

"I forgot that dads' laps could be as good as moms' laps."

COMING HOME: A SUMMARY

Warning: Hopes May Be Too High (page 128)

Make sure the children know: the parent *isn't* "all better"
Everything will *not* be back to normal immediately
There may be changes in the home: new equipment, furniture or rooms rearranged

Suggestion: Start Having Regular Family Meetings (page 129)

What to do at your first family meeting
Telling your children what to expect:
  If full recovery is likely
  If full recovery isn't going to happen

Making Plans for the Homecoming (page 131)

Get the kids involved: planning, shopping
No big parties, please
Make sure the children, especially the older ones, know they can go to a private place if they get overwhelmed
A helper in the chaos: your answering machine

Bringing teachers and schools into the picture (page 132)

What to tell them now
Once again: *no compromise on your children's performance*

A Good Idea: Keep up the regular family meetings (page 132)

Another Good Idea: Reestablish your family rules (page 133)

Important: make private time for your children, and for each other (page 133)

Watching for signs of trouble, again (page 134)

SEVEN

When It Won't Get Better

CHILDREN AND "ALWAYS"

Up until now, we've been thinking mostly about medical situations where something will *happen.* Within a time frame of weeks or months Dad's illness will get better, or it will get worse. The chemotherapy will succeed or will fail. The body will accept the transplant or reject it.

But this chapter is about a situation that is, in many ways, more difficult for everyone—for the patient, for the partner, for the children. In this chapter, the science of medicine has come to its limit, has helped as much as it will help. Now the wheelchair, the darkness, the body's betrayal of itself have become permanent. Change, if it happens, probably will not be for the better, and it will come imperceptibly—not over days and weeks, but over years.

Now we are dealing with always.

Difficult as "always" and "forever" are for adults to accept, they are far more difficult for children. A child's world is one of new ideas, new skills, new developments almost every day. The only "forevers" in your child's world are the things he's always taken for granted, never even thought about—home, family, two healthy parents. Those are the "forevers" that are changing now.

Before we can even start to consider bringing children safely through this new reality, we need a way of thinking about chronic illness and how it affects family life. There is one image that I came across years ago and that has stayed with me as I've worked with families struggling to adapt to an illness that won't get better.

Greenland

Imagine that you and your family have planned for years for a wonderful trip to France. You've studied the maps and the brochures; you've even learned a little of the language. You know all about driving through Normandy and you've packed your swimsuits for the Riviera; you're ready for Paris and the Seine and hot croissants at sidewalk cafés.

At last you and your family board the airplane and wing out across the Atlantic. The plane touches down. The attendant opens the cabin door . . .

And you're in Greenland.

What might you feel, looking out that door across an icy, alien tundra? There would be, first, a feeling of total disorientation, then, perhaps, a crushing sense of loss.

This is exactly what many families feel as they face the prospect of a parent's lifelong illness.

Yet a moment's thought will probably suggest one additional idea to you:

Even Greenland has possibilities.

Coming to Terms with Your Own Altered Future

I can promise you now, as I have in every previous situation: Your children can handle this new reality, can live and grow and *thrive* despite—and even because of—the travail of a parent's lifelong illness. In my experience, *the children usually emerge whole and sound.*

But the parents who face a chronic illness must help themselves before they can possibly help their children.

No child can adapt to your new condition if you are angry all the time, or constantly depressed, or more dependent than your medical situation compels you to be. As long as the parent is struggling against this new reality, the children will struggle and fail to adapt.

So before you can begin to help your children, you must first look at yourself.

Do you understand this new future?

Can you accept it, or at least get past the injustice of it?

Can you reach this understanding: "My life has changed, but it's going to go on"?

There is the tendency now to echo John F. Kennedy's homily: "Life is unfair." I think that puts life in terms that are far too narrow, too centered on ourselves. Life is neither fair nor unfair. Life is life. And if life takes us unexpectedly to Greenland, perhaps we can learn to ski.

Helping Your Child Come to Terms with a Different Future

What you are struggling with, your children are struggling with. Usually it's on an unconscious level; rarely will they be able to talk about it. The unexpressed feeling is: "I'm *never* going to have a dad like Dad was." Inevitably, there is a huge sense of mourning, of loss. Most of this chapter will be about getting *beyond* the mourning, accepting the loss, and living and coping with this new reality—this new emotional Greenland.

Preparing Your Children

You should proceed now in very much the same way that you did when your illness was first diagnosed, as we discussed in Chapter 1. As you face a future of living with permanent illness or disability, you must take your children into the process. Some parents are hesitant about this; they fear they might be *leaning* on their children for emotional support.

A common reaction is "I don't want to make our child think he has to solve our problems."

Quite the opposite: You are opening yourselves up so your children can *lean on you.*

You must tell them, with complete honesty, your understanding of what is coming.

- How the illness will proceed, and on what timetable.
- The plans you've made and are making for how the family will readjust and cope—who will do "the Mommy things" or "the Daddy things."
- Once again, as in Chapter 2, you and your children should plan the help you will need and expect of them.
- Very important here, your own feelings and reactions. In sharing your own uncertainties and sense of injustice, you give them permission for their own emotional responses, their grief, their rage, their sense of loss. Again, your purpose in opening yourselves in this way is *not* to gain emotional support from your children. Instead, you are offering them a *model,* an understanding that what they feel is acceptable, *because Mom and Dad feel that way too.*

The Continuing Dialog

What your children will need in this new reality is the same kind of absolute honesty and openness we've been talking about since page 1. But now they need one thing more: The dialog must continue over time.

Remember, the situation will never be static. Even if the parent's condition remains unchanged for months or years, *the child is changing every day.*

Right at the beginning, you and your children will need to talk out what has happened to Mom or Dad, the emotional impact, and how ordinary, everyday life is now going to change. But that *is* only the beginning; parents can never enjoy the feeling "Okay, we've talked it out; I've explained to them what M.S. or progressive blindness or Huntingdon's or spinal cord damage is, and what's going to happen, so *that's over.*"

Continuing the dialog is one of the most important things you can do for your growing children. As they grow, their understanding and their physical and emotional capacities grow with them. Inevitably their development will be affected by the abilities and condition of the sick parent.

Choose some regular intervals to talk, and be governed by how much the child seems to need. The parent's visits to the doctor or hospital are a good time to bring the family up to date. And watch how your children react; if you get "That's great, Mom; gimme the details later 'cause I'm late for band rehearsal," fine. Your child has put his dad's illness into the background music of his normal life.

Remember: Just because a parent has a chronic illness, that *doesn't* mean the children have a problem with it. And if you *expect* a problem, if you keep pushing information at a child who isn't particularly worried, you may create a self-fulfilling prophecy. You may get the child to *start* worrying.

Fear of the Parent

Sometimes it happens: This new, somehow "different" parent returns from the hospital and the children back away, physically or emotionally. They may not know how to handle the situation, or they may actually fear the parent.

It's important to get past that, and it's important for the child to get comfortable again with whatever level of interaction the parent can now handle.

In general, infants and toddlers adapt best to the situation. It may take a three- or four-year-old a little while to adapt to the parent's limitations but, pretty soon, if Mom can't pick Jimmy up for a cuddle, Jimmy learns to climb into Mom's lap.

The older the child, the more difficult the adaptation—the more the child fears for her own well-being, the more bad things she can imagine.

If the child is simply afraid, that's pretty easily overcome with a moderate amount of education and instruction. Before the parent comes home, tell your children exactly what to expect: how things will look, feel, smell; what special equipment may be coming home, and what it's for, and how it works; what helpers may be coming to the house. Explain the parent's condition in detail: the physical limitations, lack of stamina, emotional struggle.

Let the children approach the situation slowly, at their own pace. You can offer suggestions (which they may accept or reject):

"How about just going over and giving Mommy's hand a squeeze? I bet she'd like that."

It's important not to be shocked at a child's initial fear or reluctance and *not to make too much of it.* I've seen situations where a child gained a lot of positive reinforcement by persisting in the attitude, "Don't wanna be next to Daddy." Concerned grandparents, aunts, uncles, friends would rally around, coaxing the child to go see Daddy, talk to him, hug him. The child quickly learned that simply by *not* going to Daddy, she became the family's center of attention—and kids *love* to be the center of attention.

If you encourage the child to experiment and don't overreact, pretty soon it's likely she'll overcome her fears and reestablish a normal relationship with the parent. If that *doesn't* happen, if the fear and revulsion *don't* diminish over time, then something else is probably going on. You may need professional help to find out what's wrong and how to deal with it.

Hope, Limited

As the child looks at the parent's new limitations and begins to face up to "always," it's important to keep hope going, to find good things in the future. Your ten-year-old may have always wanted Dad to take her to Disneyland, to walk around the Magic Kingdom with her. Now Dad will never walk around Disneyland. Still, even in a wheelchair, perhaps he can take the whole family to McDonald's on Saturday. And that's a start. If he can do that, then one day, perhaps, he can *roll* around the Magic Kingdom with her.

When your child digs in, seems absolutely determined to be miserable because of what Mom or Dad *can't* do, the child is still in the stage of rejecting the new reality. So it's important to take these baby steps, find the little things the parent *can* do, to keep the family working as a family. Dad can't coach Little League any more, but he can sit in the stands and holler.

It's a matter of adjusting expectations, of finding the good in the smallest things, *and it's hard*—for you and for your children. Perhaps Mom has had a stroke, gone through rehabilitation. She can walk, a little. Her thoughts may be clouded. Her speech is slurred. Now she's home, with her new limitations.

You've had time; you've prepared the children. They know Mom will need home nursing, with health aides coming and going. Perhaps Grandma is moving in for a while to help. The children know that Mom's brain has been damaged, that the most you can look for is tiny improvements. If Mom could count to three when she came home, and today she can count to six, that's a great improvement, and the family should try to be excited by it.

Dealing with this kind of loss is terribly difficult for children, but it's part of a process. And for the process to work, the children have to *grieve* for what they've lost.

How Children Grieve

Children's grief is different from adults', and the younger the child, the more different the grieving. Young children usually don't maintain a continuing level of sadness. Instead, what you see is: happyhappyhappy*DEVASTATED!* The same child may be shrieking with laughter at a party, then go up to his room and sob heartbrokenly.

As children grow older, their grief becomes more like our own; you'll see a more mature, more level sadness as they learn to go on with their own lives despite the loss of parenting. There will be "down" moments, but not those enormous peaks and valleys of a younger child's grief.

Enabling Grief

When your child sinks into those valleys of despair, you should *give her permission to grieve,* not try to stifle the sorrow or cut it off. At those moments when you sense that your child is teetering on the edge of grief, there are ways you can *invite* the child to tears. There are so many things you can say to trigger the emotion and bring it out.

"It really hurts, doesn't it, to think of Mom like this?"

"It's just so sad, isn't it, about Daddy?"

When the tears do come, the best thing for your child is simple, physical comfort. Your instinct will be to cuddle, to soothe, and that's the right instinct *as long as you don't try to cut off the grief.*

When a child *really* cries, when he abandons himself in misery, most parents' natural inclination is to think "I want you to stop crying; I don't want you to hurt so much." But your child *does* hurt that much; you can't change that. It's simply counterproductive to say "Stop crying now. Mommy wouldn't want you to cry."

What you can do is let the hurt come out. You don't have to say a thing; just by being there and holding your child through the pain, *you're doing the best job you can possibly do.*

It may go against your instincts, but it's important to help your child work through that misery, before he can come out the other side and adjust to the new reality.

Denial

Sometimes children simply refuse to face the fact of a parent's illness and an altered future: "Nothing's sad, everything's just like it was; it's gonna be fine." And for a while, that may be okay; you can respect a child's desire to proceed at his own pace. If your child really needs *not* to think about the new reality, you might offer a nonthreatening "We're going to have to talk about the changes in our lives pretty soon," just planting a seed.

Since we're talking about a chronic situation that isn't going to change very much very soon, I'd rather go a little too slowly than too quickly in working toward children's acceptance. Open the doors for them, respect their defenses, and they will probably adapt in their own time.

But if you as a parent can't get through to your child, don't beat yourself up about it; start to think who else might be able to get through. You and your child might be *too* close at this point; perhaps he'd open up to an uncle, a cousin, the mother of a pal. Teen-agers often tell me they can talk only to their friends, because only other teens understand what they're going through. As we've said, that's perfectly normal, healthy teen behavior.

The Boy Who Got Stuck

I met recently with a fourteen-year-old boy whose father has a connective tissue disorder. The disease first struck when the boy was six or seven; the father's condition stayed about the same over the years. There was some loss of function, but he retained a great deal. He could go to work and play with his son.

Suddenly, a year ago, there was a new attack; the father underwent a series of operations. He emerged stable once more, but much weaker and more limited, far less able to engage in activities with his son.

The family tried to adjust, to take the most optimistic view: It could have been worse; Dad could have lost so much more; the doctors caught it in time; now we can look forward to Dad being no worse than he is—et cetera.

Yet the boy seemed to "get stuck"; he couldn't get past the new changes in his father. His behavior and his schoolwork both began to deteriorate.

When I began working with the young man, he wouldn't talk about his dad or almost anything else. But I knew he had one passion: a really distinguished collection of baseball cards. As soon as I began asking about baseball cards, he became animated, talking first about the cards, then about other, more active things he really liked to do, and finally about how much he wished his dad could still do those things with him. He began to bring his frustrations out in the open, to recognize his own rage at what was happening.

In their need to remain strong, to put the most positive face on the new crisis, his mother and father had never given their son the chance to say "This is bull! You *weren't* this sick before. Just when I really need to have you around as my dad, doing stuff with me, it all fell apart!"

So I asked, "Do you think you can tell your dad how you feel?"

The boy shook his head. "I could never do that," he said. *"It would hurt him too much."*

I think he was absolutely right. It was a remarkably mature and compassionate understanding. But *by talking his frustrations out with me,* he seemed to come "unstuck." He could unbottle his feelings, look at his anger, and recognize that it was both justified and acceptable.

Weeks later I ran into the boy and his mother in a drugstore. He seemed a bit shocked to see me—child life specialists don't buy hair-spray!—and hung back out of earshot. His mother told me that both the behavior and the schoolwork had improved since our talk. A little later he sort of wandered up the aisle past me and murmured, "Well—thanks for everything."

In this case I was the one who "allowed" the conversation he could never have with his father. But I think that any warm, sympathetic confidant—anyone he trusted—could have gotten the same results just by offering an attentive ear and permission to *hate* what had happened to his dad.

Affirming Their Emotions

Children do best when their parents can confirm the emotions that go along with chronic illness. The child should feel that Mom and Dad understand, that it's *okay* to resent having to stay home with Mom while the other guys are playing ball. It's okay to be mad about things like that, to think it's not fair: The other guys don't have to do things like that, *but I do.*

The child really needs that permission from you: It's okay to absolutely *hate* the fact that you have to take care of your mom. *You have to do it, but you don't have to like it.*

No matter how well your family adapts, each of you from time to time is going to have these furious, frustrated flashes: "This isn't right. This really makes me mad. This shouldn't have happened to me. *Why is it happening to me?*"

Those feelings will never completely disappear, for you or for your children. As long as you give yourselves permission to have those anguished moments, as long as you can make the struggle to get back on track and accept the reality, as long as you allow yourselves and your children those moments of despair, your family can remain whole and flourish.

Two Particularly Bad Times for Children

Most of the time, children can "float." If there is no dramatic change in a parent's illness, children adjust, adapt, and "float"—living their lives from day to day, as normally as possible under the circumstances. But there are two periods—one during latency, or school age, and one in the early teens—when your children may seem to be newly stressed by the parent's illness, *even though nothing much has changed.*

Trouble in Mid-School Age

School years are usually a pretty mellow time for kids; in this latency age they're not quite so vulnerable as they were as toddlers or will be again as teens.

But somewhere around the middle of school age—roughly, between eight and ten—something changes. At this point, children are still extremely focused on themselves, but now their peers are beginning to become important. Your children start thinking about what their pals might be thinking.

Somewhere in here you may see your child begin to struggle with having a sick or handicapped parent. She'll become much more aware of the parent's condition, hesitant to bring friends home anymore. She'll worry about what the other kids will see in her home, how they'll react to a parent who talks, acts, or looks "different."

If the child begins to fear the loss of those developing friendships, a parent's illness can now become a real, major conflict for her.

But then, after that tough year or two, things return to normal for a while. The child matures and comes to learn that her friends really aren't going to reject her because her mom or dad is "different." For several years, your child can "float" again. And then comes the second, even more touchy period of difficulty.

Trouble in Early Teens

Thirteen to fifteen is never a day at the beach, for the child or the parents. It's a time of life when your child wants to be just like all his peers, look like all his peers. He doesn't want anybody to rock his boat, and at that age it's already a pretty wobbly boat. The extra needs, the very fact of a parent's handicap can be destabilizing for the young teenager.

(Of the two "times of trouble," the early teen period may be less severe, especially if the parent's condition has existed for quite some time and the child had adjusted to it.)

Other Causes of Trouble

Beyond running into these developmental "times of trouble," a parent's continuing illness may cause problems for children when:

- There is a change in the parent's actual condition.
- There is a change in the family environment—a new job, a new town, a new home.

The Signs of Trouble

How do you know when your child is feeling these stresses, is losing the fight to "float"?

Many of the warning signs are the ones we discussed in Chapter 3, *but now they will be more subtle.* Because the parent's condition has become part of the family "background sound," children's stress reactions will show themselves more slowly, more insidiously. The child's grades won't suddenly go from As and Bs to Ds, Fs, and Incompletes. There will be a gradual decline, perhaps over several terms, in school achievement. A well-behaved child gradually becomes less well behaved; an average-behaved kid starts developing into a problem. It is important to bear something in mind:

The child's problems may have nothing to do with the parent's illness.

CHECKLIST OF WARNING SIGNS

It's a mistake to think that, just because a parent is ill, the illness is automatically the central fact of a child's life. With one child maybe it is; with another it isn't. Even with the same child, *sometimes* it is, and *sometimes* it isn't.

When a child starts developing problems or getting into trouble, you as a parent probably have a mental checklist you run through:

- Having problems with friends?
- Bad company?
- Drugs?
- First love?
- Hormonal change?
- One of those days?
- Hard year in school?
- A rough time developmentally?
- Physical problems?

There are many other possible causes. The checklist is still valid but, with a parent chronically ill, you must add one more *possibility:*

- Something about my illness?

Work it out, as you do all the other possible causes of trouble. Is the child suddenly embarrassed by the parent's condition, even though she hasn't seemed to be in the past? Is the child burdened by responsibility? Could I be asking too much, going beyond what she's ready to handle?

Don't give the illness too much weight or too little. But don't make the very common mistake of thinking that "Something about my illness" is the only or even the most important behavioral factor in your children's lives.

What Can You Do?

If you determine that your son or daughter is showing warning signs of stress, and that the parent's illness is an important factor, there are several things you can do. One is very specific.

If you suspect that your child is becoming afraid of how her friends might react to her "different" parent, it's a good idea to confront the problem head-on: Encourage her to invite a pal over to the house. And if you think that some of her circle of friends might indeed handle the situation badly, then you'll want to hand-pick the pal.

Once the two of you have decided who should come over, spend a little time with the friend; explain the parent's medical condition, and what she's going to find in your house. Just as when you took your own children to the hospital a couple of chapters ago, preparation is everything.

Great Expectations

Most parents fly by the seat of their pants, and usually that's fine. But a parent's chronic illness forces you to think:

- What is it I want for my family?
- What is a good family life?
- What do I want for my children?
- What do I believe about raising children?

Being forced to confront these questions directly is one of the good things that happen now. Because, chronic illness or no: *You should still want the same things, still have the same expectations of your children.*

You should maintain the same approaches to parenting, enforce the same discipline, distribute the same chores, require the same curfews. You children need stability and boundaries. So *all these things need to remain in place.*

That's why, when parents say to me, "How should I behave now?" I simply ask them, "How would you have behaved if this *hadn't* happened?" Just because one of you is sick, that's no reason to change your children's world.

Gains Amid the Losses

Any chronic illness, with its permanent loss of some part of the body's skills, is a tragedy. I would never dream of minimizing it; there is no place for Pollyanna, the Glad Girl, in our approach. And yet . . .

Seldom is a disaster as disastrous as it first appears. Greenland isn't *worse* than France, it's just *different.* If we can adapt to the differences, we can make this new reality valuable, even positive—particularly for our children. Sometimes we can still give them more than we think we can . . . it just takes some ingenuity.

I'm thinking of Roy Campanella. Arguably the greatest catcher in baseball when he played for the old Brooklyn Dodgers, Campanella smashed up his car one icy night in 1958 and emerged a quadriplegic. Yet every spring until he died, Roy Campanella parked his wheelchair beside the batting cage at the Los Angeles Dodgers training camp in Vero Beach and taught the young rookies how to hit. For the last thirty-five years of his life Roy Campanella couldn't even pick up a bat, but the baseball that was in his head remained a priceless asset.

A father who has lost his eyesight will never teach his daughter to drive. Yet sitting in the backseat of the car, he can tell her things she needs to know—to use the brakes *before* she turns, or that, as soon as she can see the front of the truck she's passing in her rear-view mirror, it's safe to pull back into the right-hand lane.

A parent forced into medical retirement may well be devastated, his sense of his own worth terribly diminished. And yet, over time, I've seen such parents come to another realization: "I'm here with my kids. I'm going to spend time with them during certain marvelous periods of their lives that I'd never have known without this illness."

This is not the mindless optimism of Pollyanna. It is the unsentimental, correct analysis that good things frequently do arise from the ashes of the bad.

The Computer People

I know a father, a professional man, whose son and daughter were ten and fourteen years old when he was diagnosed with multiple sclerosis.

The disease took a rapid form; just a year after the onset, he was forced to take a medical retirement, and soon he began to lose the ability to speak. Luckily, we now live in an age where there are alternative ways to communicate.

The father began using a computer, both to speak and to write.

Simply to keep up with him, the rest of the family—his wife and children—had to sharpen their own computer skills, far beyond anything you or I might be able to do. They learned all kinds of databases, spreadsheets, computer languages—just because that's what his disease was forcing *him* to learn.

The girl and boy now have tremendous computer skills at a remarkably young age—and the whole family is inordinately proud of those skills. *Of course* the disease continues its inevitable progress; *of course* the family wishes the past were still the present—yet in the midst of its struggle, the family has this really positive new thing, a direct result of the father's illness.

"A Mile in My Moccasins"

Part of being a child is the focus on self—most normal children see the world as revolving around their own needs. Only gradually, as they grow, do they learn to be more other-directed, to identify with people other than themselves. We say they learn *empathy.*

Most children are allowed to remain self-centered and self-absorbed all through those early years. They are never pushed to feel what it would really be like to be someone else, and struggling. There's no reason they should be.

But with a parent who will never get better, and may gradually get worse, children's ability to empathize becomes crucial to their own well-being and the health of the family.

At our institution, we've developed techniques that allow children, particularly school-age children, to understand—to *feel*—what life has become like for the handicapped parent. With minor adaptations, you can use the same ideas with your children and achieve the same results.

What we try to do in these group sessions is mimic the symptoms of the parent's illness in the child's body. Of course the children must *want* to play the game, and usually they do. It's interesting, it's fun, it's even funny—and it ends.

If a mother has a degenerative muscular disease like M.S., we'll tape a couple of ten-pound weights to the arms and legs of her twelve-year-old, then have him try to run around the room or build a Lego fort. He feels what it's like to live inside a body that's tired and uncoordinated.

If Mom or Dad is a paraplegic, we give the child a wheelchair to roll around in—and then tell her to go into the kitchen and scramble a couple of eggs without leaving the chair, or take herself to the bathroom.

If the parent has a visual impairment, we'll give the child a pair of glasses with distorting prisms over the lenses—or we'll just smear Vaseline thickly across the child's own specs—then ask her to find her way to the door or read some Nancy Drew aloud.

Where a parent's problem is neuromuscular, we may have the child reverse handedness—then ask him to button his shirt from the wrong side or write a letter with the wrong hand.

Where disease will impair a parent's speech function, we let the child load up his mouth with marshmallows, then ask him for directions to the cafeteria or shout a sudden, startling question at him.

You see the idea: We try to let the child *experience* what the parent is experiencing—for just a little while. With a bit of ingenuity, you can do the same thing for your children—and share a lot of laughter in the process.

Does it work?

At the end of these workshops, we ask the children what they've learned. One session recently included a quiet youngster, the eleven-year-old son of a father with the degenerative disease multiple sclerosis. After most of the other children had given their impressions, and the room had become pretty quiet, the boy suddenly spoke up. He said something like this:

"You know, if you were always able to do something, like play ball, and then all of a sudden you couldn't do it anymore, and if it was something you *really* liked to do, and you knew you'd *never* be able to do it anymore . . .

"Wow!

"It would be so frustrating. You'd just get so mad, and you'd take the mad out on everybody around you . . .

"Now I know why my dad is so mean and angry sometimes. It's because he's so frustrated. He used to be able to do all this stuff. I can get out of the wheelchair. *He can't ever get out!*"

It was remarkable to watch the boy talk his way to an understanding of what his father was going through. It was as if he had taken himself out of himself and into the heart and mind of another human being much earlier than he ever would have otherwise.

And this, I think, may be the most positive thing that can come out of a parent's chronic illness. The children can learn empathy at a much earlier age, and that ability to empathize, to feel another's pain, to "walk a mile in his moccasins," will stay with them throughout their lives.

Losing Some Childhood

There is a price to be paid for this increase in empathy, and it is an important one: the loss of some childhood.

So often a parent diagnosed with a chronic illness will say to me, "I just want my child to be a child. I don't want *my* disease to affect *her.*" My answer is always the same: *"That's not possible."*

There is no way your child can have the childhood he or she would have had if you had not become ill.

For one thing (and it is not a bad thing), your child will have to learn to become more independent. If your ten-year-old daughter really *must* have clean jeans morning, noon, and night, she'll have to learn to run the washing machine, and that's perfectly okay. It's also okay—and probably inevitable—for her to resent having to do it; all her pals' mothers do the washing for them!

The loss of childhood involves learning an equation: "If this is what you want, this is what *you* have to do." It is the price they pay for the skills they learn.

Helping Kids Help Themselves

It's always a mistake to think of children as helpless *objects,* acted upon and shaped by outside forces beyond their control. Children are bright, resilient beings capable, with only a little help from their friends, of finding their own answers, their own coping skills.

When Daddy Couldn't Help

I met a little girl named Maryanne. When she was just two and a half years old, her father was shot in the neck, damaging the spinal cord. He became a quadriplegic. How this tiny girl adjusted to her new reality is one of the most remarkable processes I have ever witnessed.

At first, Maryanne seemed utterly terrified of this strange new father. In the hospital, she didn't want to see him. When they went to visit, she'd hide behind her mom.

During those visits, we began getting together in the playroom. Maryanne didn't have a lot of verbal skills yet, but almost all her play focused on "Daddy." She'd identify a doll or toy as Daddy, then play Daddy-this, Daddy-that. She'd put the Daddy toys in different hiding places around the playroom, bury them in our rice table, then carefully retrieve them. She seemed to need the reassurance that wherever she left her toy "Daddy," that's where she would find him.

At the end of the sessions, she'd always want to take all her "Daddies" home; I'd tell her she had to pick just one and bring it back next time.

At home, her mother told me, that Daddy toy would be very important to Maryanne. She always knew exactly where the toy was. She would carry it around, then put it somewhere, then go back to check on it.

When her dad was sent on to a rehabilitation hospital, Maryanne continued to come by our playroom, play with all her toy "Daddies," take one home each time. And by the time her father came home for good, she had made the connection between the old daddy and the new one. She lost her fear. Because Daddy couldn't pick her up anymore, Maryanne would climb into his lap and give him a hug big enough for both of them. It worked for her, and it worked for him.

I'd never presume to know what goes on in the minds of very young children. But as Maryanne worked with these daddy symbols in the hospital environment, she found a way to get through her fear of this different, damaged daddy, to accept his limitations, and to reestablish her loving relationship with him. This was the magical thing she decided to do for herself, and it worked. All she needed us to give her were the tools, and the time.

On Their Own

In earlier chapters we were dealing with acute illness—a crisis that would resolve itself, for better or for worse, within a foreseeable time-frame. When your children became angry or upset, I could suggest interventions, ways you and your children could handle the crisis together.

Facing up to a parent's chronic illness—to "always"—is a little different. Yes, you can offer the support, the model, the permission to grieve and to be furious at the situation. You can guide the process and be there for them, but your children now must find the resources *within themselves* to cope with a parent's chronic illness all through the months and years of growing up.

The only strength we can rely on, to be there whenever we need it, all down the years, is the strength that comes from within. With your support, your children can and will build that internal strength of their own. And at the end of the process, you'll be proud of your rugged young Greenlanders.

EIGHT

When Things Get Very Bad

Two Fathers

Two young fathers, in adjoining beds.

I had come to see the one in the nearer bed.

He had been in his own home one morning, playing with his two children, ages five and three, when suddenly he collapsed. The children had watched as the rescue squad arrived and rushed him away to this hospital. Now he was awaiting very risky surgery for an aneurysm—a weakened blood vessel that was leaking into his brain and threatening to burst.

He might die.

His wife and I brought the children to visit. He was weak and not fully conscious. He couldn't answer them, but he could open his eyes at the sound of their voices, could see them, could smile because he loved them and because they had come. Such moments are incredibly valuable, not only for the children, but also for motivating the patient to *try.* I have seen parents on the edge of death make an effort to come back, to respond at the sound of their children's voices.

I took a Polaroid picture of them together; the children kept it.

In the next bed lay a man with a brain tumor, dying. His wife was visiting him. The man's nurse took me aside and suggested I talk with this second young mother.

The nurse had overheard the first family—she had heard the children talking to their father, heard their questions, heard their mother and me explaining that, yes, this is very serious. We just don't know how Dad will be. Yes, he could die.

What bothered this nurse was that the second young woman refused absolutely to tell her children *anything* about their father's illness and impending death.

Well, sometimes I get paid to be pushy. So when the woman had finished her visit, I took her aside and suggested some of the ideas I've been sharing with you—the children have a right to know, have the need to know, and their future may depend on your courage and honesty right now.

She was courteous, listened to all I had to say, thanked me for my concern, and told me, "The children are fine." They did not need to know their father was dying; she saw no reason to upset them. And good-bye.

We try; sometimes we fail. I've gotten philosophical about that. But the nurse was anything but philosophical; she was furious. As the mother left, the nurse told me in an angry whisper: "Do you know how hard this is for us? That man's brainstem could explode at any time. He and his children had a chance for something important—their last time with him—and their mother says they are fine!"

Last Things and First Things

If you have turned to this chapter, it means we will have to talk of last things and first things. There is no easy way to write it; there is no easy way to read it. So I will try to do for you what I told you, all those pages ago, you must do for your children: Be absolutely honest.

My qualification to speak to you now is this: I have held the hands of many dying friends, and I know of their going, and of the children they left behind. The purpose of this chapter is still the purpose of the book: to help your children emerge from crisis mentally, emotionally, and spiritually whole. But I know, beyond any doubt, that in helping your children into the future, you will help yourself into that future as well.

Is It Ever Too Late?

Whatever has happened with your children up to this point, I come back to one very central point: It is *almost* never too late to start doing things the right way.

Here is when it was too late:

The nurse called from intensive care: A young mother was there, in the last stages of pancreatic cancer. She had hours, perhaps less, to live. Her children, a teen-age girl and boy, were coming in from out of town. But what the nurse told me next, I could hardly believe:

They didn't even know their mother had cancer.

I went to the unit and met with the father. He was devastated. Obviously, he loved his wife deeply and was agonized at the thought of losing her. Yet in the six months of her disease, he had told the children as little as possible, had never *used* the word "cancer." He said they'd never asked him any questions; their lives seemed fine, and he didn't really think they needed to know anything. He himself had obviously spent the past six months in pretty serious denial, refusing to accept even the possibility that his wife might die.

By this time my heart was aching: for him, of course, but especially for the children. *Six months* knowing their mother was ill, guessing frantically, with no freedom to talk to anyone. And now—now it *was* too late. *There was so little we could do.*

What the father wanted us to do was very simple: He wanted somebody else to tell his children their mother was dying.

The children came in. I sat with them in our conference room; their dad came in too. He was willing to be there, but he just couldn't say the words.

I remember the two teen-agers were almost silent, their heads bent; no eye contact anywhere.

I said, "You must be wondering why we had you come here." They nodded their heads, without raising them.

"You know your mom is sick. Do you know what she has?" They shrugged. It was just so hard.

Finally I had to tell them: Their mom was right on the verge of death. They could see her, but it would have to be now—she would probably die within the hour.

They fell apart. They cried, they sobbed, doubled over in anguish, doing in that moment all the grieving they'd been denied for half a year.

They chose not to see their mother before she died.

And afterward, I remember the father saying:

"I don't think I did this right."

I don't know what "this" was, in his mind. But I believe it was a very generic statement about the entire six months: He was saying, for his whole family, "*We didn't make the time valuable.*"

So: However much time there is now, *there is time.* Let's see how we can make it valuable.

Helping Yourselves, Helping Your Children

First, let's talk for a moment about you: you the sick parent and you the well parent. You're going through the very worst of times now, and it would be just plain silly to talk about helping your children without suggesting that, *first,* you must help yourselves. Because you are so overwhelmed with the demands on both of you. Because you are dealing with rising tides of anger and confusion, of hope and no-hope. So sometimes the needs of your children must take a back seat to those intense feelings, those pressures, *and that's okay,* that's *normal.*

That is why so often, when I'm asked to help a family's children, I work first with the parents. They are so distraught, they *can't* think about their children until they settle their own emotions. So I give them all the time they need to talk about how tired they are (and they are), how unfair all of this is (and it is):

"We just got our life started . . ."

"We waited so long . . ."

"We bought a new house . . ."

"We moved to a new community for its marvelous schools . . ."

"This just isn't right!"

The parents must get all of this out, look at it and learn to get past it, or at least live with it, before they can really help their children.

How Children Come to Terms

Normally, in children—and in adults too—the possibility of a loved one's death arises gradually, almost silently. The long medical process of treatment, of hope, of fear; of upturn, then downturn, gradually leads to the loss of hope that the parent can recover.

It's a terribly difficult time for the children, because both parents become more and more ambivalent about talking to them, about keeping them informed. The parents, of course, don't want to admit the possibility of death *even to themselves;* how can they possibly admit it to their children?

Remember: *Your children always know when something is happening.* They won't know in detail; they may not realize that what has happened is that death has become possible. But your children have very delicate antennae for picking up mood. When optimism becomes pessimism, *they will know.* When you begin to exclude them from unhappy truths, *they will know.* They will have an increasing sense that something is *not* being said. And it is always better for them to know the facts than to sink deeper and deeper into uncertainty and fear of the unknown.

As the prospects grow darker, your children may be uncomfortable asking questions; now you must take the initiative. With older children, when the parent's medical situation grows worse, I usually ask the question: *"How much do you want to know?"*

It's a question that's perfectly safe for you, or a counselor, or a friend to ask. Some children answer, "Don't talk to me about bad things," but they're the minority. In my experience, *most children want to know what's going on.*

I remember how one little boy answered my question. He never talked much, yet he'd shown me right along that he understood: His mother was really sick. He had told me she could die. I told him the people at the hospital were going to try a lot of ways to keep that from happening. But, I asked, if things get very bad, do you want us to tell you? How much information do you like to have? Do you like to hear everything, or just a little bit? He thought about that, then he said: "I think I want you to tell me everything—*but sometimes I don't want to talk about it.*"

It was such a perfect answer—such a good description of what so many children feel.

You may be comfortable deciding for yourself exactly what and how to tell your children about a deteriorating medical situation. But if you feel uncertain, it helps to run your ideas by a professional you trust—a hospital psychologist or social worker: "Should I tell him this? Can she handle that?"

Regular family meetings are really useful now. Your children know that on Thursday night they can sit down with you and ask for the latest information from the hospital.

When to Push It

Keep in mind: A child's *failure* to ask questions *doesn't* necessarily mean there's something wrong. Looking away may be this child's style of dealing with stress: "Be happy, mon." The well parent's job is to keep the door open for conversation when the child is ready: "Anything you want to ask about Mom? Well, whenever you're ready, we'll talk."

But when something dramatic is about to happen—when a serious illness becomes grave or terminal—then you should begin to push past the child's defenses; the child *must* have advance warning that things are about to become very bad. It will go against your protective instincts as a parent; the information may be terribly upsetting for your child. Nevertheless, he'll be better able to cope at the end if he's had time to anticipate, and to work through the pain of what's coming.

Painful as it is, the information should be clear and straightforward:

"Honey, Mom isn't coming home from the hospital this time. We think Mom is going to die."

There may be no immediate response. Children throw up protective shields against such devastating news. Acceptance is a *process.*

If possible—if death is not a matter of moments—then try to respect that protective mechanism. Give the child time to accept.

I've seen children hear words like "We think Dad will probably die; the doctors say there's nothing more they can do," who've responded, "Oh. Okay." And go on as if they hadn't heard. And hours later—that night—the next day—they burst into tears, acknowledging that they *did* hear, all those hours ago, but weren't ready to handle it. Perhaps the hospital environment wasn't safe for them, perhaps they needed privacy or the presence of a certain person to comfort them.

It's okay to repeat the message, to try to get through again.

But if your child completely blocks the information, refuses over time to react or even acknowledge that he understands what's happening, then you should seek the help of a counselor or psychologist. A trained professional can help you get through the child's defenses—and can also determine when the stress is becoming too much for the child, and you must back off.

Helping Children to Feel

At this point, nothing is more important than letting your children know how *you* feel. You must have the courage to drop your own defenses.

The Little Boy Who Wouldn't Listen

The grandparents brought the two grandchildren to the hospital. Their daughter, the children's mother, had had a brain aneurysm—a burst blood vessel. Surgery had failed. She was on a ventilator and now it was going to be turned off.

She was a single parent; no husband in the picture. The grandparents, midwestern farm stock, loved their only daughter deeply—but they were determined to be strong.

We started talking about turning off the ventilator and what that would mean. The older child listened intently, but the five-year-old boy kept trying to change the subject, trying to distract us, running around the room. Finally he simply covered his ears.

I took the grandfather aside. I told him I was sure the little boy understood what was happening but was pretending with all his might that he didn't. And I said, "*It has to be okay with you if he cries.* You have to show him how *you* feel; he needs this permission from a man, someone he respects."

We went back into the room; I asked the grandfather to take the little boy on his lap—I wasn't going to continue until somebody was holding that child.

Then I started, once again, to talk about the mother's condition. I explained what had happened to his mom—that her brain had died, and the rest of her was about to die too. I try to explain clearly and in great detail, so the family can use the explanation when the children ask questions in the future—as they will.

I thought the boy was going to cover his ears again, but this time he listened.

Finally he looked up and met my eyes. I still didn't know whether I was getting through. I said, "You know, everyone around here is really, really sad, even your grandpa. Grandpa doesn't show his sadness very much."

At that moment, his grandfather began to cry. The little boy looked at him, saw his tears, and said, "No, no, not my mom!" And then his own tears came.

They cried and cried; we all did. But this child just needed that permission; he needed to see that it really was okay to start feeling this, and that there would be someone there to hold him when he did start feeling it.

That little boy did not need stoicism and strength. He needed to see vulnerability and grief so that he too could be vulnerable and grieve.

To know you have reached your children, to be sure they understand, you must get an emotional response—and *your* emotional response will be their guide.

Some children can grieve without crying, but not many. And there is no "right amount" of grief. *The cause of the pain comes out in the tears.* When they are ready to stop, they will stop. Probably they will sleep.

Final Communications

As I look back, so much of this book has been about communication—the flow of information and emotion within the circle of well parent, ill parent, and children. Now we'll begin to think about final communications within the family—the ones that must last your children a lifetime.

"Are You Going to Heaven?"

I'd like to tell you the story behind the picture on the next page.

I was working with a hospitalized mother who knew she was terminally ill. She had one child, a daughter of about fourteen. She wanted to prepare her daughter for her own death, and yet she couldn't talk about it. She was afraid, I think, both for her child and for herself.

They both liked pictures, loved colors.

One day I suggested they do a picture together. The daughter didn't think much of the idea.

"Mo-om, I'm really too old for this kind of thing."

But I gave the mother a handful of brightly tinted Magic Markers, and she began idly to sketch some colored lines. It wasn't a picture, really, just noodling around.

After a while, the teen-ager said, "That's kind of pretty, it looks like a rainbow," and picked up a couple of markers to make more lines. In a few more moments, Mom said, "Now what does it make you think of?"

Her daughter said, "It looks like heaven." And then she said, "Mom? Are you going to heaven?"

And then they began to talk about death: Mom's death. And they both agreed they were both pretty scared. They decided that what their painting needed was a little boat, to carry Mom to heaven.

As communication, it was almost accidental. And it was perfect.

There was no longer any shadow of fear or misunderstanding: Mother and daughter were together, looking at the future, which was a wash of brilliant colors and a little black boat.

"I'm Not Sure Dad Can Handle That"

Many families, I find, raise barriers of miscommunication in these days of crisis, in a mistaken effort to "protect" a child or a parent.

I remember a young mother whose uterine cancer had recurred. Treatment had failed; medically, there was nothing more to be done. She looked extremely sick, and no one knew exactly how much time remained. Her husband and three children were devastated, the way people are devastated when hopes are raised, then dashed. The husband told me he didn't think his wife understood that she was dying: "She can't handle this, I don't think."

So he felt he couldn't tell their children. It would be disloyal while his wife still kept hoping. He thought it important now that the family do fun things together, but that the children mustn't talk about death. And I told him children can do that.

He and his mother had brought the three children to the hospital, and I said I'd be glad to meet with them. At this point, the grandmother suddenly said: "I think Suzanne needs to see you *today.*" And the fourteen-year-old nodded.

We walked down the long corridor to a private room. Suzanne needed to talk. And one of the first things that came out was "Mom's going to die, isn't she?"

She said, "I keep thinking about all the things I'm not going to have now, all the times that Mom's not going to be there anymore. My school trips. Graduation. When I get married." I realized, Suzanne was *practicing,* was getting herself ready for a future without her mother, and doing it alone, and courageously.

So I told her: "Your dad doesn't think Mom knows she's dying."

And Suzanne said indignantly: "But she does. She *told* me she was dying!"

It seems that one day after the cancer recurred, Suzanne was helping her mother into the tub, and her mother said, "Know what? I don't think I'm going to make it this time, baby. I think I'm dying."

I asked Suzanne, "Do you think we can tell your dad that?" She was uncertain. She said, "I'm not sure Dad can handle that."

The mother is home now, and we've all been working to bridge the gap. She and her husband seem to be talking more, making plans, but the d-word still hasn't passed between them. They're getting to it. Gradually, I think, they will all arrive at the truth together.

Messages to the Future

A few chapters ago, we talked about messages—little surprise notes and presents while Mom or Dad is in the hospital, to let the children know that, even though you're sick, you love them and think about them. That kind of message can continue into your children's future. It is at once the most difficult and the most rewarding effort in a parent's final time.

Some parents write notes; some make audiotapes. We haven't done videotapes, but that's another possibility.

And it doesn't require a whole lot: You know what the landmarks will be in your children's lives, the important moments when you might not be there. Pick just one or a few:

- The first day of junior high or high school
- Bar mitzvah
- Confirmation
- High school or college graduation
- Engagement
- Marriage
- Birth of a child

You can leave messages of love and encouragement for any one, or all.

Some parents hesitate, wondering whether such messages from the past won't simply reopen old wounds, recall a sorrow left behind many years ago. The pain of "Yes, Mom was thinking of me—*but I'll never see her again.*"

My answer to them is this: The important part of the message is *Mom was thinking of me.*

It does cause pain, but it does *not* wrench open old wounds. Almost invariably, I have found, the message is positive. When a growing child, or young adult, learns that Mom or Dad left them a special message, they do feel the loss again, at a reduced level, *but they also feel the love again.* It strengthens the ego: Mom or Dad really loved me, *and I am a lovable person.* He or she cared so much, in those last days so many years ago, to think of me right at the very end!

People tell me: "It was so hard to read, so sad, but he loved me enough to do it, and I was so glad. *I could almost hear his voice.*"

So write or speak the message. Think about your two-year-old son, and what you'll want to tell him when, at thirteen, he becomes a man in the Temple. Hold your six-year-old daughter in your mind, and tell her what you'd like her to know on the day your first grandchild is born.

Making the Effort

This is something the well parent can and should help with, because it takes an effort. It's hard, *hard,* to look beyond your own personal tragedy into your children's future without you. A grave illness must turn our thoughts inward, to this personal catastrophe, yet messages to the future require that we turn our thoughts to others—to our children—in the midst of our own anguish. And the well parent is the best one to say "I know it's hard to think about. But important things are going to happen in Julie's life, in Danny's, and *they're going to need your help and guidance.* Can we talk about some of those things?"

Some parents simply cannot do it. And if they can't, they can't. I find the situation, for some reason, is a great deal more difficult for men. Fathers leave messages far less often than mothers do, and that's a tragedy. So many women have told me, despairingly, "I tried and tried to get him to write or talk into a tape recorder; he just couldn't do it."

I find it's also harder for a well husband to suggest such legacies to a gravely ill wife.

Of course, there are exceptions; some fathers leave wonderful spoken legacies for their children; some mothers simply can't. In the end, it is an extremely personal decision. All I can do is tell you what I am certain of: Such messages to the future will be good for your children and good for you.

When mothers or fathers leave these messages, they almost always experience an enormous sense of release, of *completion.* There is a glow about them, the kind of glow you see at births and at weddings. And the sense of completeness comes to the well spouse too. One father told me, after listening to his wife's taped message: "I don't know if this is more important for the children or for me."

A Message

I remember a young mother who wanted to leave a message for her six-year-old daughter, but she said, "I just can't write." Then she began telling me about the day her daughter was born, and all it meant to her.

I produced a little tape recorder and said, "Maybe you could just talk." Well, she tried; nothing would come. I said, "Would it help if I ask questions?"

So I started the tape, explaining to the little girl that Mom is thinking about her and wants her to hear her thoughts some time in the future. Then I asked one or two questions, and the mother's thoughts began to flow, and I didn't have to speak again.

She was a little teary at first, but then, as she spoke on, her voice grew very calm and spiritual. She said:

> *I wish I could be with you on your wedding day. But I guess nobody ever knows when they can be with their children. I was thinking of how you'll look the day you get married. Did you ever see the picture of me in my wedding dress, that Dad has? If you haven't seen it, you should ask him to show it to you.*
>
> *I hope the man you're marrying is someone you really love . . .*

It was just very sweet. She talked about the good times and the bad times. She said:

> *You know, Dad and I used to have some fights; we'd get so mad at each other, we'd wonder why we got married. But we always patched them up. And then when you came along, it was so special: it made us a whole* family.

By this time I was teary, but she was very calm. Once she got going, she spoke to the tape for ten or fifteen minutes, and then stopped and said, "I don't know what else to say."

I said, "I don't think there's anything else you need to say."

She never recorded another message. She died three years ago, but her daughter has a wonderful legacy in her future.

What to Say

Here are some other things I've heard parents leave behind:

Almost always, there's an expression of love. Some parents try to leave a spiritual explanation, or interpretation, of their death. Some can talk about the imminence of death; some cannot.

Many will share religious beliefs: "I believe I have been a good person; I believe good people go to heaven. We learned that in church together. And that's where I think I'm going to be." And some will go on, and tell their children what they think heaven, or the life beyond death, will be like.

What *Not* to Say

But be a little careful. Some of this can be scary.

I wince when a parent tells her children something like: "I'll be watching over you. And if you do something bad, *I'm going to know it.* So don't disappoint me."

That kind of concrete warning can make children feel constantly guilty, can cast its shadow on their lives far into the future, can cloud their judgment and undermine their egos. And if there is time left, I try to help the parent see the risk of that kind of message.

If the parent is close to the end, and this may be the very last message, then I don't interfere—but I try to work with the child afterward, to make that message a little less concrete, a little less fearsome.

Messages: One More Thought

In a way, our children are our own message to the future; they are our immortality. So the greatest tragedy is not to die before our children; it is to outlive them. And this tragedy, now, is avoided.

We pass that message in two forms. The qualities about us that won us the love of our mates, our children—the curl of a smile, or the way our eyes can laugh, or a squinchy new way of seeing things, or the love in our own hearts—go on in our children, taking wonderful new forms in each new twist of the genetic spiral. And so those legacies of ourselves will spiral down, through the years and the generations. It's totally out of our control; that's *why* it's wonderful.

The second form of the message is what we say and do, what our children learn, both from what we try to teach them and from the way they see us conduct our lives. This is the message over which we *do* have control, right to the end and, if we wish to make the effort now, beyond the end.

So, however great the effort of sending these final messages—and the effort *is great*—the result, I believe, is worth it.

Last Days

We're going to look at two different situations: where a parent is able to spend the last days at home, with the family, and where those days are spent in a hospital.

The Hospital: Final Visits

As we discussed in Chapter 5, the most important part of a visit to a very sick parent is *preparation.* Particularly if the child hasn't seen Mom or Dad for a while, she's got to be put on notice *in advance* as to what she's going to see. The key object is the same: If the child is going to have a strong emotional reaction, have that reaction in a safe place, *not in the hospital room.*

Again I'd suggest the use of Polaroid pictures to show the child what Mom looks like now and to explain all that sometimes-frightening medical equipment surrounding her. The older the child, the more careful the preparation must be; somehow younger children seem to *accept* these situations more readily than their older siblings.

After the preparation, the decision must be the child's own. Most younger children, I find, want to make these final visits; older children are more ambivalent. The important thing to remember is this: Whatever decision the child makes is right for that child, *providing that the child makes it.*

With late-stage hospital visits, as with funerals, I find that the parent frequently puts pressure on the children on the basis of his own earlier experiences. If, as a child, he was denied a final visit to his own dying parent, or if he was compelled, unwillingly, to peer at a dead parent in a casket, he may very well try to press his own child to the other extreme.

Remember: If the child wants to visit a parent at the end, that's all right. If not, *that's all right too.* And if you don't like the child's decision, don't press. He may very well change his mind, or vacillate back and forth, and you can work with that. But:

If the child wants to visit and isn't allowed to, or if the child *doesn't* want to visit and is compelled to, that can cause lasting trauma and real anger in the child. Now is the time to let the grieving happen, not to block it with anger and hostility.

"I Never Had a Chance to Say Goodbye"

One source of anger that I encounter repeatedly in children long after a parent's death, and even in adults many years later, is this single despairing sentence:

"I never had a chance to say goodbye."

So without exerting excessive pressure, it is probably wise to freely offer a final visit to a dying parent. And if the child does want to visit, it's probably *not* wise to discourage it. Because the anger of that moment, of "I never had a chance to say goodbye," can leave a lasting emotional scar. The emotion of anger blocks the emotion of grief, prevents grief from happening. And what is vital when a child loses a beloved parent, is to allow the child to grieve, and so get beyond the loss.

But what of the child who really *doesn't* want make that last visit?

"Something to Remember Me By"

It's important to offer alternatives. Any but the youngest child is going to feel some guilt, deciding not to visit an extremely ill father or mother. So let's find surrogates for the visit—little things the child can send in place of himself.

Sometimes we pick flowers; I promise the child I'll put them in a vase, right where Mom can see them. Or I ask the child whether he'd like to draw a picture or write a poem, as a message to Mom; I'll show it to her, read it to her, tape it to the wall.

Whether children visit the parent or not, *they need a response.* And that's the job of the well parent, because the sick one probably can't do it:

"Daddy's pretty tired now, but he thinks you drew a *beautiful* picture of all of us; he's got it right there on his wall."

If the sick parent can still respond, then that's going to be a very valuable interaction, an important memory for the child in the future, and usually the child will want it.

What If the Parent Says No?

Sometimes it happens that the children want to make these final visits, and one parent or the other rejects the idea. Usually it's the well parent; sometimes it's the sick one. In either case, the rationale is something like:

"I don't want them to see me (or see Mom) like this."

"I don't want them to remember me (or her) this way."

"I don't want them to be frightened."

It's not often in this book that I've *urged* you to do something, but now I urge you: *Put this attitude aside.* What your children will gain from these last visits (if *they* want to make them) will far outweigh any hypothetical harm to them.

The children need the closure of these last times together. The physical situation may be daunting, may be frightening, but your children *can* get past it. They're trying to reach the real parent whom they love, within that depleted physical shell. And simply by making the decision to go visit, they are already setting themselves up for the experience, saying "Yes, we can handle it."

PREPARATION

After that, once again, it's simply a matter of preparation. Look back at Chapter 5 and how we prepared them for a visit to a critical-care unit. Tell them exactly what they're going to see; if there's going to be an emotional reaction, let it happen at home where it's safe, *not* in the critical-care unit.

The Polaroid photo can now help everybody. If the sick parent is hesitant, if she doesn't "want them to see me this way," then suggest the photo as a halfway step: "How about this: I'll show both kids the picture, and ask if they still want to come visit. If they say yes, you'll know they're ready to handle it."

These last visits are worth the effort they involve.

(I've been asked what happens when a dying parent wishes to see his or her children, and the children don't want to go. In my experience, *that has never happened.* Whenever the parent has been conscious, capable of communicating, the children have wanted to visit and say good-bye.)

If the parent can no longer communicate, the children have to be prepared for that lack of response. Often I tell them, "Even if Mom can't talk to you, or say thank you, somewhere inside her heart, the place where she keeps her feelings, she knows that you're here, that you're trying to help, and she appreciates it."

I tell them that because I believe it. I believe it is true even when a parent is unconscious, or on a ventilator, or deeply sedated, or comatose. Somewhere inside she knows her children have come, and is grateful.

The Very Last Visit

Even after death, there may be the question of a final visit to the bedside. About half the children, in my experience, want to go in. With the younger children, the toddlers under three or four, I don't encourage a visit to a parent who has died. Their concept of death simply isn't clear enough for such a visit to have meaning. *They don't understand that the body isn't alive anymore.*

But it's still important to offer the other options—to ask whether they'd like you to leave a picture, a poem, a flower, or some special token beside Mom.

I know a family where the father's work involves a great deal of travel. He never leaves home without a little box containing one token—a toy, a barrette, a little charm—from each child and one from his wife. It's magical thinking, and it works for this family; the children have no doubt they're keeping Dad safe while he's away, and I suspect Dad thinks so too. Something like that may help your family now.

It's very normal for children to vacillate at this point: They are confronting life's final mystery. They want to see Mom, they don't want to see Mom. So at some point that seems right to you, you must be strong enough to say: "It's time for us to go home now and make some plans. So this is your last chance to see Mom while she's here in the hospital. If you'd like to do that, it's still okay; but if not, it's time for us to go home."

Last Days at Home

Given our choice, most of us would prefer to spend our final time at home, and, more and more often, that is what is happening. It's a good and humane development.

Another good and humane development of our times can be your family's best friend now: the hospice. Once the possibility of medical treatment is at an end, *no one* should leave a hospital without hospice referrals.

Most hospitals are now affiliated with hospices, and your hospital social worker can put you in touch with one. In an outpatient situation, your physician, nurse, or social worker can refer you. In a pinch, you can find hospices listed in the Yellow Pages.

The basic guideline for a hospice usually is that the patient have less than six months to live. When hospice people know that a child is in the home and may be involved in caring for the patient, they work very hard with that child. They'll explain what medical situations may arise and how to handle them.

You'll find your children are probably more receptive to descriptions of the processes of dying than adults are; generally, *children aren't as afraid to think about it.*

If possible, try to avoid the situation where your child is alone for any extended periods with a dying parent; try to have someone else in the house. But if that's impossible, your child *must* understand the process of dying; that's where the hospice teaching comes in.

The Good Days

I will tell you that these final days can be very good days indeed.

I'm thinking of a man, in the terminal phase of cancer. He was divorced, but his ex-wife suggested that he now move back in with her and their fifteen-year-old daughter. It was a warm and generous thing for her to do. At the time all this happened, he was growing weaker but could still get out occasionally. Whenever he did that, he wore a hat; the chemotherapy had left him entirely bald.

A hospice was involved, helping the family to deal with the prospect of death, explaining just how things would happen. One day when I was meeting father and daughter, she said, "What I'm really scared of is that I'll be there alone with you when it comes, *and I won't know what to do.*"

This is what her father told her. "If that happens, *I want you to do nothing heroic.* I just want you to stay with me, and talk to me, and tell me that you love me. I don't want you to call 911. I just want you to stay with me."

And they agreed on that. Then the father said, "But I'm not dead yet. What we have to do is plan our time together."

The girl thought for a little while. She said, "The most important thing in my life now is getting my driver's license."

We nodded.

She said, "You're a better driver than Mom."

Dad nodded.

She said, "So that's what we could do together: You could give me a driving lesson!"

The father wasn't at all sure that was such a good idea in his debilitated condition. But the girl had it all figured out. "Come on! If a cop stops us, you just tell him you're dying of cancer! He'll never give you a ticket! And if he doesn't believe you—well, just take off your hat!"

And, the following Saturday, that's what they did. I'm not sure it's the strangest parting gift I've ever heard of, but it was surely one of the neatest.

As to the kind of help your children can provide for a parent who does come home, I'd suggest referring back to the list we worked out in Chapter 2—with special attention to how your own family style affects what should and shouldn't be asked of them.

Facing Death: How Children React

The way your children react to the prospect of a parent's death is going to surprise you, the well parent. And not all the surprises are going to be pleasant.

Remember that a child's world is absolutely centered on himself. Only as we grow toward adulthood do we gain the ability to see through others' eyes, walk the mile in someone else's moccasins.

CATHY'S PLAN

I remember five-year-old Cathy, who started telling me, with great composure, exactly what was going to happen after Mommy died. She announced firmly, "I want Daddy to find me a new mommy and get married again. And I want to have a baby sister; I want to be a big sister. So I want my new mommy to have a baby."

I told all that to Cathy's father (who laughed and shook his head), and explained that this is very normal for a child her age. Actually, I said, what it showed me was the security you and your wife have provided for her. It's not that she doesn't love her mom, and it's not that she thinks you could transfer your affections so easily; that's not what this is all about. *She's five,* and she's very clear about what she needs in life, and *what she sees herself as needing is a mommy and a daddy and a baby.* So she's just going to arrange the world to get those things, which is what five-year-olds do.

He laughed again, so I told him that if Cathy brings it up, you can just tell her that you're not ready yet to get her a new mommy. But don't be surprised or hurt if she says it. *It's not an indication of a problem.* It's good stuff, not bad stuff.

Many children tell me they've thought, well before a parent dies, about having a step-parent. Usually the idea surfaces about the time they first realize the parent is seriously ill. And school-age youngsters tend to have reactions that are the polar opposite of preschoolers. These older children tend to become really angry when they think about a step-parent. One nine-year-old told me, "The one thing I'd be so mad about, after my dad dies, is for my mom to get married again. *She's never going to get married again.*"

The important thing to remember, as your children begin to look toward the future, is that every family is unique, and every child will respond in his own way. There are no hard-and-fast rules as to what is the proper response and what isn't; there are only guidelines. And the first guideline is that the child works outward from his own needs.

The Question

At some point, your children will ask it: WHY?

I won't pretend to help with an answer; we each must find our own. All I can do is warn you: It is coming, and you must be ready for it.

Some families, in my experience, understand their own beliefs in great detail. Most do not. Now it will become important for you to know, coherently, what your own faith believes about death and what follows. Here is where your clergy can be of enormous help, in providing not only the comfort of faith, but also the detailed instruction from that faith, which you can give to your children.

I've dealt with families of every denomination: families who believe in a joyous afterlife and families who believe in none; Jewish families who tell me a loved one lives on in the people who loved her; and Buddhists who explain reincarnation to me and their children. Sometimes, if a child asks me "Why?" I will turn the question around and ask: "What do you think? Why does God do the things He or She does?"

Usually I find that children have some beginnings of an explanation, based on what they've learned at home and at church and in life.

You must be prepared to deal with fury and despair. Children have told me, "I think God is terrible, and I don't want to believe in God anymore." I acknowledge that, tell them, "It sounds like you're really angry at God, like you really blame God for all this." And I suggest that, after a while, the child talk it out with the family priest, minister, rabbi, or counselor.

Sometimes children just want to lash out, and I tell them, "I understand how mad you must be, not only at God, but everybody you think had anything to do with why your mom is dying . . . the doctors, the nurses, the other driver, the car maker, the cigarette company."

Usually, I find, children will give in to their feelings and then leave the need for explanation behind them. "Life is unfair." And that's fine;

it's useful for them. And there really is no final explanation for why we ebb and flow as we do.

How Children Grieve

If you were to come to my office at this point, I would give you a short essay called "The Grief of Children." It was written by Susan Woolsey, associate director of the Maryland SIDS Information and Counseling Project, and is the best concise summary I know of how children process the terrible tragedy of a parent's death and how the surviving parent can help them through. Copies of the essay are available through the National SIDS Resource Center, 2070 Chain Bridge Road, Suite 450, Vienna, VA 22182 (telephone: 703-821-8955), but I want to reprint it for you here:

The Grief of Children

One of the most difficult tasks following the death of a loved one is discussing and explaining the death with children in the family. This task is even more distressing when the parents are in the midst of their own grief.

Because many adults have problems dealing with death they assume that children cannot cope with it. They may try to protect children by leaving them out of the discussions and rituals associated with the death. Thus, children may feel anxious, bewildered, and alone. They may be left on their own to seek answers to their questions at a time when they most need the help and reassurance of those around them.

All children will be affected in some way by a death in the family. Above all, children who are too young for explanations need love from the significant people in their lives to maintain their own security. Young children may not verbalize their feelings about a death in the family. Holding back their feelings because they are so overwhelming, the children may appear to be unaffected. It is more common for them to express their feelings through behavior and play. Regardless of this ability or inability to express themselves, children do *grieve, often very deeply.*

SOME COMMON EXPRESSIONS OF CHILDREN'S GRIEF

Experts have determined that those in grief pass through four major emotions; fear, anger, guilt, and sadness. It should be remembered that everyone who is touched by a death experiences these emotions to some degree—grandparents, friends, physicians, nurses, and children. Each adult and child's reactions to death are individual in nature. Some common reactions are:

- SHOCK

  The child may not believe the death really happened and will act as though it did not. This is usually because the thought of death is too overwhelming.
- PHYSICAL SYMPTOMS

  The child may have various complaints such as headache or stomachache and fear that he too will die.
- ANGER

  Being mostly concerned with his own needs, the child may be angry at the person who died because he feels he has been left "all alone" or that God didn't "make the person well."
- GUILT

  The child may think that he caused the death by having been angry with the person who died, or he may feel responsible for not having been "better" in some way.
- ANXIETY and FEAR

  The child may wonder who will take care of him now or fear that some other person he loves will die. He may cling to his parents or ask other people who play an important role in his life if they love him.
- REGRESSION

  The child may revert to behaviors he had previously outgrown, such as bed-wetting or thumbsucking.
- SADNESS

  The child may show a decrease in activity—being "too quiet."

It is important to remember that all of the reactions outlined above are normal expressions of grief in children. In the grief process, time is an important factor. Experts have said that six months after a significant death in a child's life, normal routine should be resuming. If the child's reaction seems to be prolonged, seeking professional advice of those who are familiar with the child (e.g., teachers, pediatricians, clergy) may be helpful.

Explanations That may not Help

Outlined below are explanations that adults may give a child hoping to explain why a person they loved has died. Unfortunately, simple but dishonest answers can only serve to increase the fear and uncertainty that the child is feeling. Children tend to be very literal—if an adult says that "Grandpa died because he was old and tired" the child may wonder when he too will be too old; he certainly gets tired—what is tired enough to die?

- *"Grandma will sleep in peace forever."* This explanation may result in the child's fear of going to bed or to sleep.
- *"It is God's will."* The child will not understand a God who takes a loved one because He needs that person Himself; or "*God took him because he was so good.*" The child may decide to be bad so God won't take him too.
- *"Daddy went on a long trip and won't be back for a long time."* The child may wonder why the person left without saying goodbye. Eventually he will realize Daddy isn't coming back and feel that something he did caused Daddy to leave.
- *"John was sick and went to the hospital where he died."* The child will need an explanation about "little" and "big" sicknesses. Otherwise, he may be extremely fearful if he or someone he loves has to go to the hospital in the future.

Ways to Help Children

As in all situations, the best way to deal with children is honestly. Talk to the child in a language that he can understand. Remember to listen to the child and try to understand what the child is saying and, just as important, what he's not saying. Children need to feel that the death is an open subject and that they can express their thoughts or questions as they arise. Below are just a few ways adults can help children face the death of someone close to them:

THE CHILD'S FIRST CONCERN MAY BE "WHO WILL TAKE CARE OF ME NOW?"

- Maintain usual routines as much as possible.
- Show affection, and assure the child that those who love him still do and that they *will* take care of him.

THE CHILD WILL PROBABLY HAVE MANY QUESTIONS AND MAY NEED TO ASK THEM AGAIN AND AGAIN.

- Encourage the child to ask questions and give honest, simple answers that can be understood. Repeated questions require patience and continued expression of caring.
- Answers should be based on the needs the child seems to be expressing, not necessarily on the exact words used.

THE CHILD WILL NOT KNOW APPROPRIATE BEHAVIOR FOR THE SITUATION

- Encourage the child to talk about his feelings and share with him how you feel. You are a model for how one expresses feelings. It is helpful to cry. It is not helpful to be told how one should or should not feel.
- Allow the child to express his caring for you. Loving is giving *and* taking.

THE CHILD MAY FEAR THAT HE ALSO MAY DIE OR THAT HE SOMEHOW CAUSED THE DEATH.

- Reassure the child about the cause of the death and explain that any thoughts he may have had about the person who died did *not* cause the death.
- Reassure him that this does *not* mean someone else he loves is likely to die soon.

THE CHILD MAY WISH TO BE A PART OF THE FAMILY RITUALS.

- Explain these to him and include him in deciding how he will participate. Remember that he should be prepared beforehand, told what to expect, and have a supporting adult with him. Do not force him to do anything he doesn't feel comfortable doing.

THE CHILD MAY SHOW REGRESSIVE BEHAVIOR

- A common reaction to stress is to revert to an earlier stage of development. (For example, a child may begin thumbsucking, or bed-wetting; or may need to go back into diapers or have a bottle for a time). Support the child in this and keep in mind that these regressions are temporary.

Adults can help prepare a child to deal with future losses of those who are significant by helping the child handle smaller losses through sharing their feelings when a pet dies or when death is discussed in a story or on television.

In helping children understand and cope with death, remember four key concepts: be loving, be accepting, be truthful, and be consistent.

Restarting Life

The days immediately following a loved one's death are a period of shock for the entire family. There is the funeral to be taken care of, paperwork, the routine of loss. The family goes through this period more or less on autopilot.

Then it is time to go back to life: to work, to school.

That transition, children tell me, is really hard. It's just easier not to face the routines of life again.

Returning to School

Most children say that when they go back to school, they feel *singled out.* There's a sign dangling somewhere: HIS MOM DIED. They feel the other kids are all talking about them, and they're going to be treated differently. And there's some truth to it: *Everybody knows, and nobody knows what to say.*

Earlier in this book we met Annie Marks, whose Mom died of cancer when Annie was nine. Annie found it helped to write about her mother's death, and this is what she remembered about returning to school two weeks later:

"It was really hard to go back . . . *I felt like the only girl whose mother ever died.*"

So now we need help from the school, and we need to help the school as well.

Someone from the family should go to the school in advance, before the child returns, to talk with all the teachers involved as well as the guidance counselor and the nurse. They will need to know just what has happened and how to help the child ease back into normal school life.

It's good for a teacher to say "I'm sorry about your mom. And if you ever want to talk about it, we can." It's particularly valuable for another child who's suffered a similar loss to offer to share: "My dad died too, if you ever want to hear what it was like for me when it happened."

But what is vitally important, and what the teachers must be told to encourage, is that the other children *start treating this child as normally as possible.*

They should call him by his old nicknames, draw him back into sports, band, clubs, silly jokes, and just hanging out.

Sometimes the child is going to "lose it," suddenly burst into tears. The teacher should not ignore that, but also should not make the child the center of attention. Ask the teacher, when it happens, to excuse the child with a quiet "Would you like to go down to the office? To the nurse?" Most children would rather be out of the classroom, out of the eyes of their peers, while they pull themselves together. The teacher will help the child most by acknowledging what's happening, handling it, *not* making a big deal.

Failure *Still* Not Permitted

Above all, there must be *no permission to fail.* Impress on the teachers that you expect them to demand that your child perform to his full capacity. There must be no misplaced compassion, no, "Well, no wonder she's flunking exams, poor thing."

If the child has been out of school for a significant period of time, she will have difficulty coming back up to speed; even a good student will require special attention and coaching. Marginal students need a *lot* of help to get back on the track; school is not the release and pleasure for them that it is for the good student. Nevertheless, expectations of full performance must continue, both from the teachers and from the family. *Permission to fail now can mean the start of a lifetime pattern of failure.*

As long as the teachers and staff are notified in advance, I've found most schools to be very helpful, very concerned with getting the child past the tragedy. Some schools even have trained crisis teams: counselors who meet and talk with the child on the very first day back. The school can be your best ally now; lean on it.

Keep Looking for Trouble

As you and your children begin adjusting to this life after death, you will probably find they return to normal faster than you do: It's the nature of youth to put the past away and grow quickly toward the future.

Nevertheless, keep watching for those signs of trouble we looked at in Chapter 3:

- Sleep disturbance
- Eating disturbance
- Fear and anxiety
- Aggressive play
- Patterns of failure
- The quiet child
- Risky behavior

As always, you are the expert; you simply have to pay attention. When you think something is wrong, *something is wrong.* And by now you know what you can deal with yourself and when you need a little help from your friends.

A Personal Note: To the Parent Who Is Still Here

Now is the hardest time. Probably the worst thing that will ever happen to you has just happened. The dear partner of your life is gone. And now, here comes a stranger, a child life specialist sitting in a distant city, to tell you that you must begin to look outward—to share this terrible grief—for the good of your children.

And yes, that is what I am telling you. And I do it with a clear conscience, for two reasons.

As you know better than anyone in the world, the central concern now of the wife or husband whom you loved so much would be for the health—physical, mental, emotional—of your children. Children who emerge from this tragedy whole and sound will be your last, best memorial to your absent friend.

And the help you can give your children in *their* grieving will help you in turn. Certainly the wrenching sadness will not go away, yet sharing it with your children will make good things happen *within* the sadness. You will support each other, become closer, and emerge stronger—a family still. And that too is what your absent friend would wish.

NINE

Dealing with Special Family and Medical Circumstances

There are some special circumstances—family and medical—that affect how we apply the guidelines set forth in the preceding chapters. Special family situations include:

- The single parent
- When the patient isn't the parent

The special medical situations we'll look at include:

- AIDS
- Mental illness
- Hereditary disease
- When the child *did* have a role in causing the crisis

If Yours Is a Single-Parent Family

Many of the stories in this book involve single-parent families. Working with so many single parents who've faced serious illness, I've learned two things:

- Everything in this book that applies to children in two-parent families applies equally, or even more strongly, to children being raised by a single parent.
- There are special conditions that apply uniquely to a single parent who faces a medical crisis. Those are what we'll look at now.

Remember that for children growing up with only one parent in their lives, things become very murky and worrisome when that parent becomes ill. One of childhood's most basic concerns is security: "Who'll take care of me? Who'll do the 'Mom things'?"

Find Someone to Be the "Well Parent"

For the two-parent family, there's a sort of automatic backup system in place—the "well parent" who can take over some, or most, or all the roles of the sick parent. The first thing for you the single parent to do now as you face a major illness is to try to find someone who can fill that role of "well parent." It may be your own mother, a brother, sister, or cousin, your closest friend, the mother of your child's playmate—someone you know will stick with you and your kids through whatever is coming.

This does not have to be the person you'd want to raise your children if you were no longer with them. Perhaps you'd plan for them to go to your own parents, who live in another city. But *right now* you want someone close and *close by,* available to you and your children on a continuous basis. Make it clear that you're asking for their help *only* through the course of the illness; they're taking no responsibility beyond that, no matter what the outcome.

It's important for that helper to know as much as you now know about bringing your children through your crisis. So I would urge you to give this book to the helping relative or friend, and ask that he or she read at least those parts that directly bear on your own situation. The less you feel up to reading, the more he or she should read.

Your helper should be alert for the early warning signs of a troubled child (Ch. 3) and be aware of the kind of help that can be provided within the family's own circle, as well as the levels of help available on the outside (Ch. 4).

Make Long-Term Arrangements for the Care of the Children

You've probably done some thinking about it, even made some preliminary arrangements. Every single parent has in the back of her mind the auto accident, the sudden illness that could leave her children in a world without her.

But now, with a medical crisis, the situation is imminent. Hard as it is to do—and it's far harder in the face of your own illness—you must think the situation through and get the machinery started. Even if your condition is very treatable, and you have every expectation of coming through with colors flying, now you *must* make the unsentimental analysis: "If something happens to me, what do I want for my children?"

Remember: By *not* deciding, you are making a decision—and it's probably not a good one. Without an advance plan, your children may wind up at the mercy of *whoever decides to fight over them*—the courts, the welfare system, a former spouse. Even though legal considerations are beyond the scope of this book, I would urge you to consult a lawyer, to make sure that your wishes for your children's future will be carried out.

Custody issues, the rights of a divorced parent, child welfare laws all are far beyond the competence of even the most caring hospital social worker. Every state has its own rules, and you need professional guidance through the minefield. This kind of planning, with legal assistance, will ensure your children's security—and your own.

And now you are ready to reassure your children, to answer the questions that your illness has raised about their future.

Tell Your Kids About the Plans You're Making

"If Something Happens to Me . . ."

First, be assured: *It is not frightening for a child to hear those words.*

Our children are exposed to ideas of violence, change, and death from the time they start watching cartoons on television. You aren't giving your child any new idea when you say "If something happens to me . . ." All children in all lands and times have worried about the illness or death of a parent, and America's children today probably know more—and worry more—than any other generation.

So when you, as a single parent, tell your children, "If something happens to me . . ." and then go on to explain the arrangements you've made for them, *you're not scaring them, you're reassuring them.*

Choose the time and place carefully; this is deep and emotive stuff for your children. At some point when you discuss the illness with them, and you begin to probe for their fears, the subject will probably come up on its own: "Who'll take care of us?"

Here's the kind of thing you might say then:

"If something does happen to me, you guys are all set. You'll be living with Aunt Ellen. She loves you very much, and she's promised she'll take care of you just the same as her own kids. We've talked it over, and she knows just what I want for you."

Then you can reassure them, by explaining what you truly believe. If you feel you will beat this thing, survive, prevail, then tell them so: "I expect to be with you a long time. I plan to be here until you grow up, until you have grandchildren for me. These plans are just in case."

But even if the prognosis is bad, even if you think that perhaps you won't make it through, you can be honest and still be positive and reassuring for your kids:

"I intend to be with you guys just as long as I can. One of my biggest goals in fighting this disease is to have as much time with my family as I possibly can. You're the reason I'm fighting so hard."

Remember, even if they don't bring it out in the open, the question of the future is surely there inside their heads. So it's up to you to go fishing, gently:

"Do you worry sometimes about who'll take care of you?"

"Want to know some plans I've set up, just in case?"

The timing is up to you. You don't want to use this book like a cookbook: "Well, she says I've got to talk to them about it, so here we go, right in the middle of dinner." You'll feel when the time is right—when your children ask, or too obviously don't ask, "Who'll take care of us?"

I can't tell you *when* to share these plans; I can only explain how important it is that you *do* share them with your children. Let me say it once more: By raising the issue, "If something happens to me," you will *not* be scaring your kids. You'll be *unscaring* them.

Reassuring Younger Children

Probably, for the younger kids, that will be enough. From toddlers up through early school age—seven, eight, or so—children simply want to be reassured and then go on about their business. If you tell them confidently that Auntie Ellen, who loves them a lot, has promised to take care of them, that's probably all they'll need. Young children usually don't want to have a lot of input about planning the future; they're content as long as *you've* done the planning.

If you do encounter a strong negative reaction, if your young child announces, "Don't *want* to be with Auntie Ellen," or "I *hate* Uncle Phil," pay attention to that; something real is probably going on. This is different from "Don't want to go; want to stay with *you,*" which is a perfectly normal reaction. But if the child understands that you're talking only about a time when you might not be here, and still objects strongly to the guardian you've chosen, better do some more thinking. It doesn't *necessarily* mean anything inappropriate is going on with Auntie Ellen or Uncle Phil; perhaps Uncle Phil inadvertently frightened the child somehow, years ago.

But whether anything is really "wrong" or not, how much chance is there that a child with such negative feelings can ever develop a good relationship with her new guardians?

Reassuring Older Children

Beginning with the later school years—around age nine, ten, or eleven—children *do* want to have an input into your plans for them, and they're entitled to it. That doesn't necessarily mean you'll accept their wishes, but you owe them a hearing.

You'll probably find they have very strong feelings about where they'll go and who'll take care of them, if you're not here. And (surprise!) the people they'd pick for their primary caretakers may not be the people you'd pick at all.

Think through, carefully, your children's wishes. Their ideas may be quite good, or totally inappropriate. Your fifteen-year-old daughter may want to go live with the most permissive of your sisters—the one who, in your view, lets her girls get away with murder. In that sort of situation, address the problem directly. Say:

"I know you'd like to live with Aunt Sylvia. I know you like the rules she has for her kids. But you know those aren't my rules. And what I need is to make sure that you guys continue to grow up with the rules *I* believe in. That's my job as a good parent. You may not like it, but that's what I need to do for you."

Doing What's Best for the Child

There will probably be a lot of family pressures—some overt, some in your own mind—affecting your decisions now. Many parents, in my experience, feel obligated to name a certain individual, or at least a blood relative, as their children's guardian, *even though there's somebody else who they think would do a better job.*

The decision, of course, is yours, as the pressures are yours. In my own view, however, the children are primary here, and all the other considerations are secondary. When parents talk to me about these family obligations, I tell them they should do *whatever they think is best for the child.*

Your mother may think she *should* take the children, but a grandparent in her seventies may simply not be up to coping with a houseful of toddlers or teens. And, in fact, the grandparent may not really be thrilled with the idea. So those dear friends who are doing such a super job with their own children, and who'd love to have your kids if something should happen to you, may be the best answer for everybody. The real question should be: Is it the best answer for my children?

When Parents Are Divorced

If you are divorced, your illness may now bring your former spouse back into the family picture, at least temporarily. Be aware: The change can be both confusing and difficult for your children.

You both must be careful how the divorced parent reenters the scene, so your children don't begin to erect a dangerous structure of false hopes. Perhaps the divorced parent may envision some permanent role, may plan (with your approval) to care for the children if you become too ill. If so, fine.

But if the return is temporary—Dad coming to help out for a week or two, with no intention of a longer-term commitment—*it's crucial that the children understand.* Both parents must give a very clear message from the start: Daddy's going to be here only for this week, while Mommy has her operation. After that, he's going back to his new family. Daddy still loves you, but *Daddy and Mommy don't love each other again.*

If the children don't understand this, then *Dad's second departure will be as traumatic as his first.* Your children will go through two divorces, not just one.

And, assuming the children would want the other parent back in their lives, you must both be careful that your illness doesn't begin to take on positive aspects for them.

Younger children in particular may make the connection Mommy-being-sick with Daddy-coming-back. Then your illness *may seem an acceptable price to pay.* The child may think along the lines, "It's worth Mommy being sick to have Daddy back." Again, you must both make clear from the start: The situation is temporary. Daddy is *not* back to stay.

When It's Not the Parent Who Gets Sick

One nice thing about kids: They love a lot of people.

Parents frequently ask me what they should do when someone who is not a parent, but is close to their children, is stricken with a serious illness, or dies, or goes out of their children's lives in some other way. I may hear that it's "just" a cousin or "just" the mother of a friend; Should we be worried about the children? My answer is this.

The title doesn't matter: "Grandpa" or "Nanny" or "Mrs. Baxter in the third grade" or "Cousin Joe" or "Tommy's mommy." If that person has had a strong, loving relationship with your child, and particularly if he or she has been involved in caring for your child, then that person's illness, death, or departure from the scene is going to have an impact—perhaps even comparable to the loss of a parent. And everything we've said about warning signs, about your children's need for emotional support, and about giving and getting help will apply.

The illness or death of another child—a playmate or sibling—raises questions beyond the scope of this book. Many of the same principles—hospital visits, children's ways of grieving, preparing them for the inevitable, their perceptions of death—will still apply. But there will be additional issues that do *not* arise when the loss involves an adult. If your child loses a close friend or a sibling, you may feel the need of professional help and guidance.

AIDS

In many ways, AIDS today is what cancer was thirty or forty years ago. Back then, the news that you had cancer could well mean you would be ostracized by family and friends and that your children would be shunned and isolated.

For cancer, thank goodness, all that has now changed. Your breast tumor is a personal crisis, but it won't cost your children their friendships or their desks at school. Even the idea is ridiculous.

Yet that's where AIDS is today.

I spoke recently with a young woman whose husband had just died of AIDS. As the disease developed, she had told her children their father had blood problems, he had a tumor, he had pneumonia—all quite true. But she had never said the word: AIDS. This is what she told me:

"If I tell my children the name of their father's disease, and they tell a friend, and it gets out into the community, *my children will be ostracized.* They'll lose their friends, they'll lose all the support they need to handle what they've already lost: their father."

As we spoke, I became convinced that this was no figment of her imagination. From what she told me about her family, her community, and what had happened to another relative when AIDS appeared, I decided that her grim analysis was probably correct. It is, unfortunately, correct for many, if not most, communities today. If your neighbors found out there was AIDS in your household, would they forbid their children to play with yours? Almost certainly.

Then what do you do?

There are two dangers to be balanced:

1. **Do you keep the secret, and take a chance that your children will find out that you're withholding crucial information from them and will lose the faith they must have in you?**
2. **Or do you name the disease, giving them information that they may not be able to handle on their own, may talk about to a friend or neighbor, and risk their being cut off from the support they need?**

It is the first issue we raised in this book: openness and honesty with your children. And with AIDS, this issue is the toughest it will ever be.

There are no absolute answers; you're going to have to make some judgments. Here are some of the things to consider.

Consider the Age of Your Children

There's probably no reason to use the word "AIDS" with a toddler or young school child. It's all right to do what this young woman did: Explain that something is wrong with Daddy's blood or that he has pneumonia. The information is accurate, but you avoid the danger of giving a young child a word he may not understand and may repeat outside the family circle.

But an older school-age child, or a teen-ager, has by now been through a lot of education, in school and outside of it, on sexually transmitted diseases. Hearing the symptoms of AIDS, this child will begin to put it together. Whether he asks you directly or not, he'll be wondering inside: Is it AIDS?

Consider Who Already Knows

Another factor in deciding what and how much to tell your child is this: Who already knows?

If just one or two of you within the immediate family know that a parent has AIDS, then the secret may remain a secret. But the more people within the family who know, the more likely it is that your children are going to find out.

What If They Ask?

Your decision on how much to tell your child depends on your own assessment of his maturity and his ability to keep a family secret. But what if he asks, flat-out: "Does Dad have AIDS?"

A mother whose husband now has AIDS asked me what I would tell their children if they asked me the question. I told her flatly: "I can't lie to them." She gasped and shook her head. And I said, "Don't you think if they ask me directly, it means that at some level they know, or at least suspect?"

She said, "Well, yes, I didn't think of that. If they ask, it means they must have heard something, or guessed something."

I told her, "If they ask the question, you can be sure that what's going on in their heads is worse than anything we can tell them."

If your child asks you directly, "Does Dad (or Mom) have AIDS?" you have no option. *You have to tell the truth.* But then immediately, before the child can get away somewhere, you should follow up:

"What does that mean to you?

"When I say 'yes, it's AIDS,' what do you understand about this disease?

"Why did you ask? Is this an idea that came to you, or have you heard something? What have you heard?"

Your emphasis, in this instant follow-up, should be something like this:

"Because people don't understand this disease, it scares them. Because the disease scares people, they don't always treat you very well when they know there's AIDS in your family. So *this needs to be a family secret right now.*

"If you feel the need to talk about it, you can talk to me, or to (brother, uncle, whoever is already privy to the truth). But if you tell your friend about it, and your friend tells her mom, her mom might be scared and might not let her play with you anymore."

You should explain the realities of AIDS:

It's not easy to catch. You can't get it from eating off Daddy's plate or from Daddy kissing you. *There is no way you can harm your friends.* But because people are scared of it, because it's very, very serious, and because they don't really understand, *this is our family secret.*

Family Secrets

With AIDS, as with any disease that has ramifications in the community—for example, mental illness or tuberculosis—it's all right to provide information a little more slowly for your children and to be careful who finds out. It's still not all right—it's *never* all right—to lie to your children, but it *is* all right to keep the information a private family matter and to do whatever is necessary to maintain that privacy.

The fact is, most children are very good at secrets. Kids love to talk, yet when family secrecy is involved they can maintain the most amazing silences for incredible periods of time. Sometimes it's very sad that they do; children can keep the secrets of parental alcoholism and parental abuse for years or for lifetimes. Nevertheless, a child who can keep the secret of an alcoholic parent can keep the secret that a parent has AIDS.

Children will go to great lengths to protect their parents. And if that means keeping a deep secret and talking about it only within the family, they will do it.

What Will Happen When Children Find Out It's AIDS?

Almost inevitably, children who learn that one parent has AIDS will go on to two further questions for the other parent:

1. **"Do You Have It Too?"**

   Tell them your best current information. If you've had your blood tested, are you HIV positive or negative? What prognosis have the doctors given you? Be ready with answers to all those what-if? questions your children will have about their future security: who'll take care of them, what arrangements have you made for their future "just in case"? The more concrete and specific you can make that uncertain future, the better for your children's well-being.

2. **"Everybody Dies of AIDS, Don't They?"**

   You can deal with this as we dealt with the issues of death in Chapter 8. You can give them hope, because there *is* hope. Yes, right now AIDS is a fatal disease. But we have this time

together now, and new treatments are extending that time, are helping AIDS patients live a *lot* longer than before.

And it is fair and reasonable to talk about the *potential* for a cure. Be perfectly clear: There is no cure today. Nevertheless, scientists all over the world are working on AIDS, and someday it may well be curable. Next century, next year, next week—who knows? In the meantime, we'll try to make the very best use of the time we all still have together.

Mental Illness

Mental illness ranks very close to AIDS as a socially unacceptable disease. A parent who suffers from mental illness, who requires periodic hospitalization, who may need to take medication for years or a lifetime, adds huge complications to the task of being honest with your children.

Many of your considerations will be the same as for AIDS: Is it safe to tell people in my community about this? How many people know about this? Can we keep it a family secret? Do we want to?

Mental illness is probably a little safer to talk about than AIDS. If you decide to let your children talk outside the family's inner circle, it should always be referred to as what it is, an *illness*:

My dad has a mental illness.

- It makes him very depressed.
- Sometimes it makes him irritable, or nervous.
- He doesn't always know whom he's talking to or what people are saying to him.

Encourage the child to describe in simple, accurate terms what's going on. Depression is by far the most common form.

Of course you will give your children the hope that is there. They must know that mental illness is a *chronic illness that never goes away completely.* Nevertheless, there are now lots of treatments, more almost every day, that can help many mentally ill people lead pretty normal lives.

Much of the treatment nowadays involves medicine. If Mom is chronically depressed, she'll probably have to take medicine for the rest of her life, or at least for a very long time. She'll probably be seeing doctors regularly and may be hospitalized from time to time. But: All that treatment can help her and you lead lives with happiness and love, let you all do the things together that families do.

Offering Reassurance About Mental Illness

Your children will need the same reassurances you give for physical illness:

- Nothing you ever did made me get it.
- You can't catch it from me. (A little later we'll talk about diseases that may be hereditary.)
- Here's who'll take care of you, who will do "the Mommy-things" or "the Daddy-things."

With mental illness, the first reassurance is the most important one. For whatever reason, *the child's greatest need is to know he had nothing to do with causing it.* This is where children seem to be most fragile. So you'll want to explain very clearly that nobody "causes" a mental illness. We don't really know much about what causes it, whether it "runs in families," whether it will ever go away altogether. What we do know is a lot of things that can help, and those are the things we're going to do.

WHAT IF YOU *CAN* "CATCH IT"?

One of the reassurances we offered children about parental illness in Chapter 1 is: "You can't get it from me." We were talking then about conditions such as cancer, for which the reassurance is perfectly true.

But there are two special medical situations where the reassurance either doesn't apply or has to be modified:

- Contagious disease
- Hereditary disease

Contagious Disease

We're seeing a resurgence in America of some serious contagious diseases; tuberculosis is a good example. Children usually begin to understand the idea of contagion, of a disease that is "catching," somewhere in their early school years, around age seven, eight, or nine. They know that if Timmy has a cold, and Timmy sneezes near you, you can catch his cold.

Before this age, up through the toddler years, you can enforce any quarantine rules without much explanation: Wear a mask when you're with Daddy; don't touch his plates or utensils, whatever. But when your child is ready, you'll want to explain contagious disease and the rules it requires:

- How the disease is caused: by microscopic living creatures called germs or by tiny packets of disease called viruses.
- How the disease is transmitted: through the air, or through physical contact, or through the blood, or whatever the mechanisms may be.

You'll explain whatever rules of hygiene or quarantine are required; usually these are very straightforward and easy for children to learn. You'll also tell your children that, of course, there are no absolute guarantees about a disease that's "catching." But usually, if you're really careful, then you're safe. So that's what we'll be: really careful.

Hereditary Disease

If there's a possibility that the parent's illness—physical or mental—may be inheritable, you'll need to begin to deal with that in the later school years, sometime around the ages of ten, eleven, or twelve. That's when children can begin to comprehend the ideas of genetics and inheritance.

You can begin with simple, highly visible genetic concepts: If Mommy has blue eyes, and Daddy has brown eyes, why are Davey's eyes brown? Genetics is an exploding field of knowledge today, and there are a lot of good books to help children understand it.

Then you'll explain the specific problem involved. African Americans may carry the gene for sickle cell anemia; your family may have a history of cystic fibrosis, and so on. *If the parent has an inheritable disease, it's important to tell your children honestly: Somewhere down the road you or your own children may develop the same disease.*

The immediate follow-up is: Here are the things that we and the doctors are going to do to keep you as safe as we possibly can. This may involve genetic testing now; it may require periodic blood tests, hospitalization—whatever is necessary to prevent the disease, or to treat it early, so that symptoms are held to the very minimum possible.

And again, this is one medical field where new knowledge is arriving almost every day. The ongoing Human Genome Project promises enormous new understanding and a panoply of new treatments for a host of genetic diseases within the next few years. You can tell your child honestly: A hereditary disease that can only be treated today may well be curable tomorrow.

If the Child *Is* Involved

Very rarely there will be an exception to the basic reassurance that "Nothing you ever did made me get (this condition)." If a child *did* have some role in bringing on an accident—shenanigans in the car that caused Mom to crash, or banging into a ladder that made Dad fall off—then a different kind of reassurance is called for.

The child is going to feel great guilt and great fear. She knows she didn't *mean* to make it happen, but it *did* happen, and the consequences now are serious, perhaps lifelong.

What can you say?

You can acknowledge, and forgive.

There's no blinking the central fact: Something the child did has hurt Mom or Dad, maybe forever. The child knows that. Now she must get past it.

You can tell her, with perfect honesty: Mom and I both know *you didn't mean for it to happen.* We *know* you didn't mean to hurt her. It was an accident. Accidents do happen, that's why we call them accidents.

And second: There is no way Mom will love you any less because this accident happened. There is no way Mom or I would have chosen *not* to have you as our kid, even though she got hurt. Mom still loves you very much. She's not going to come home from the hospital and be mad at you, and not love you anymore.

You can't deny the accident, and that's not what your child needs from you now. What she needs is the reassurance of your continuing, unconditional love.

Remember the Circles of Help

Any of these very sensitive special situations may stress your child beyond your own ability to help. Your best guides are the early warning signs in Chapter 3 and, should you need them, the widening circles of help described in Chapter 4.

SPECIAL CIRCUMSTANCES: A SUMMARY

Epilogue

Way back at the beginning of Chapter 1, when we were first talking about the need for absolute honesty with your children, I said this:

Your children are affected by everything that happens in the family. The more serious the situation, the more they will be impacted.

In order to help your children, you *must* accept that basic principle. And you do, or you wouldn't still be with me, here at the end.

So we know you are going to be there for your children, keeping an eye on them, watching their behavior, assessing their responses, seeking help for them when they need it.

You recognize that when a child shows negative behavioral or emotional responses to a family medical crisis, it doesn't mean there's anything *wrong* with your child; quite the opposite. It is a signal that the situation, or the stress, or the unknown has *exceeded your child's ability to cope.* Your child hasn't become a bad person, or a mentally disturbed person. He or she is still *normal,* and is *responding normally to an abnormal situation.*

As a child life specialist, these are my central beliefs, validated by all my years of work with families like your own:

- Your children are basically good.
- Your children are basically healthy.

- Your children *want* to handle crises in the most positive way possible.
- Your children can stretch their abilities to new and unexpected levels in the face of a family problem.

Nevertheless, when dangerous stresses come into the lives of children, they can produce negative or unhealthy responses.

This book is about helping you and your children develop some *alternative* responses. The aim is for your children to build a whole new repertoire of responses—safe, *healthy* ways of coping with the wrenching, abnormal situation of a parent's grave illness. Whatever transpires now for you, the parents, you want your children to emerge whole, fulfilled, and ready for the rest of their lives.

I am always struck that parenting is so *primal,* locked so deep within our genes. I know the pain parents feel when their parenting is interrupted. I understand the fear that your children might not have you around as they grow up, the fear of the ways your illness or death may impact on the rest of their lives. A parent's serious illness leaves both you and your children feeling so *vulnerable.*

For any family to let me, a stranger, into its circle in such a time of vulnerability—to let me come to know the parents and the children—to allow me some input that may smooth the process a little, may reduce the pain a little—this is for me an enormous privilege. Now, by accepting this book, you too have granted me that privilege, and for that I thank you.

And I will ask you the same favor I ask of the families I work with in person. This book is the fruit of their experience; each family has added something to this body of knowledge and understanding. So I would like to hear from you about your own experience:

- What ideas from this book have worked for you and your family?
- What ideas *haven't* worked, and why do you think they haven't?
- What have you learned on your own, dealing with your family medical crisis, that might help other families in future editions of this book?

Please send your ideas, observations, suggestions, and comments to me c/o St. Martin's Press, Inc.
175 Fifth Avenue
New York, N.Y. 10010

Kathleen McCue
Cleveland

Calvin and Hobbes by Bill Watterson

Index